Most country doctors would feel that they had more than enough to do merely looking after their patients. As readers of Arthur Jackson's previous two books will know, however, he has never been able to resist a challenge. Having married while still a student, he and his wife Ruth have produced four children in as many years, bought a huge old Suffolk manor house they couldn't afford and started breeding rare waterfowl to pay for the house. They also manufacture portable incubators, and Dr Jackson is assistant at the local hospital.

G000061125

By the same author

TALES FROM A COUNTRY PRACTICE
MORE TALES FROM A COUNTRY PRACTICE

ARTHUR JACKSON

Futher Tales of a Country Practice

SPHERE BOOKS LIMITED

A SPHERE BOOK

First published 1989 by Souvenir Press Ltd
Published by Sphere Books 1990

Copyright © 1989 by Souvenir Press Ltd

All rights reserved.
No part of this publication may be reproduced,
stored in a retrieval system, or transmitted, in any
form or by any means without the prior
permission in writing of the publisher, nor be
otherwise circulated in any form of binding or
cover other than that in which it is published and
without a similar condition including this
condition being imposed on the subsequent
purchaser.

Printed and bound in Great Britain by
Richard Clay Ltd, Bungay, Suffolk

ISBN 0 7474 0565 4

Sphere Books Ltd
A Division of
Macdonald & Co (Publishers) Ltd
Orbit House, 1 New Fetter Lane, London EC4A 1AR
A member of Maxwell Macmillan Pergamon Publishing Corporation

This book is for the other women in my life – my daughter and my three daughters-in-law. Although none of them are mentioned in it, they have all helped correct my memory, kept me supplied with coffee, and generally brightened my existence.

This is a true story of a part of my life. The events that happened have a basis in reality, but the characters are composites of many people I have met along the way, not necessarily in the context in which they appear.

The medical events described are the bread and butter of general practice; they happen to someone, somewhere, every day.

If any of my friends, or patients, or indeed those who have had any connection with my farming activities, think that they recognise themselves or each other, I am flattered, but they are mistaken. The only real people are my wife and children, and even they have assumed names.

1

It wasn't as if I needed it, and now, having agreed to buy it, I dared not go home.

It was no use groaning, 'What have I done?' for, indisputably, it had been done. I had signed my name on the sale deed and written out a cheque for more money than I had ever possessed.

I had bought something that we didn't need, couldn't afford, and had no idea what to do with.

I had bought the farm next door to our house.

After the sale, I had telephoned my wife, Ruth. Her silence had been more eloquent than any condemnation, and now I had to go home and face her. Worse still, I was already late for lunch and, having taken time off to attend the sale, still had most of my morning visits to do, as well as the hospital round and evening surgery.

Her views had the cold logic of common sense. I debated whether to go straight home, face my devastated wife and eat my burned, dried-up lunch, or to finish off my morning's work, dispense with lunch, and not get home till after evening surgery.

Slowly I got into my car and drove home. None of my visits were that urgent.

How could I tell her that it was all the will of fate, a divine providence over which I had but little control?

I was a doctor, a general practitioner, with a busy and increasing country practice, and for some seven years I had also been the clinical assistant to the obstetric department of our local hospital. This high-sounding title really meant that I was on call for the panics: most of the babies that I delivered were urgent emergencies, often in the middle of the night.

For the latter two of those seven years, I had taken on the medical side of the hospital as well. Fred, the visiting consultant physician, came over from Norwich twice a week, and for the rest of the time we got on with it. It was a busy life.

Home was a large manor house, full of growing children. Four were our own; the rest, their visiting friends. We had six acres of garden and a lake.

Throughout our married life we had lived on the wrong side of Micawber's sixpence – always in debt and trying to pay it off. On the lake, we had developed a flock of ornamental ducks and geese. Breeding these had become more a way of life than a business, but we desperately needed the money from the sale of the young birds to pay the ever increasing bills.

It seemed that there was a tide of events that flowed strongly on, carrying me with it, helpless and protesting. It had all begun so simply: we had bought this beautiful old country house, with its six acres and lake. The ducks had followed naturally.

Desperation for the necessary money to maintain the house, the ducks, and our children had led me to develop a portable incubator, in order to fetch duck eggs home from Iceland. The catastrophic inadequacy of any commercial incubator then on the market had also provoked the construction of my own. Now, with the Wildfowl Trust using both the portable and the big incubators very successfully, there was a steady stream of potential buyers calling at my door.

It seemed that the same tide that had carried me through ducks and incubators was sweeping me into the farm next door.

This farm was land that had once gone with our old house – it practically surrounded it. It was owned by the gouty and newly knighted Sir Percival, who was retiring and moving away to live with his sisters. Having sold his

8

own house sufficiently well to finance his retirement, he had hoped to persuade us to restore the dignity of his former ancestral home (our house) by re-acquiring for it its old home farm. We acknowledged that any interest we showed could but raise the sale price for him, but at the same time he had sown seeds of desire. Had he not approached us, peddling his dream, we would not have dreamed of it either.

The farm had until recently been wholly planted with old, gnarled, worn-out apple trees. Sir Percival, with the aid of his nephew, had ripped out most of the trees and replanted the fields with many varieties of other fruit. The cost of doing so, combined with the loss of income from the uprooted old trees, had forced the nephew to seek his fortune elsewhere, and had persuaded Sir Percival to sell up and retire.

He was well known to our friendly bank manager, who had taken my idle enquiry about finance seriously, and produced from head office official sanction to lend me the money. At the time I had merely been performing a routine follow-up blood test, checking his full recovery from jaundice. The enquiry was conversational, idle, in passing; I had been more concerned with my answer to his inevitable question as to when he could start drinking again. He had not asked me. We had talked only of the fruit farm next door.

The solicitor involved had reported to the surgery for a routine tetanus injection. Offers for the farm were to be made in sealed envelopes. While the solicitor was apprehensively lowering his trousers, prior to the injection, I had distracted attention from the impending assault on his person by asking him about the procedure for a sealed envelope bid. While replacing his trousers – and his dignity – he had offered to act for me in the matter, and attend the auction.

There it would have rested, had not old Miss Havers

developed bronchitis on the morning of the sale. She lived next door to the solicitor's office. My car was parked outside it.

This tide, that was sweeping me on, diverted my footsteps. I should have opened my car door, climbed in and driven off. I didn't. I walked up the steps to the solicitor's office, and opened the door.

He was in the hall, just inside the door. I was whisked off to the auction where, on my behalf, the solicitor bought the farm, lock, stock and barrel.

I signed the deed of sale, wrote out that gigantic-sized cheque, and walked out of the room.

To try to rationalise my actions, listing one event after the other, only produced a very lame excuse.

At any point I could have said 'No' and walked away. Subconsciously I must have wanted it, have needed the extra work and worry of five more employees, and forty acres of fruit farm. Consciously, I knew that I must be an idiot – an opinion my wife would endorse as soon as I arrived home. But at the same time, I was elated. I realised we did want it.

Ever since Sir Percy had informed us of his intention to sell the farm, we had discussed the possibility of buying it and, for every sane reason in the book, decided that we would not do so. We couldn't afford it, we didn't need it, we knew nothing of fruit growing, we had too much to do already. Every conceivable logical reason was against it – and yet, first thing every morning, having got out of bed, we walked to the window and looked out over it; last thing at night, we pulled back the curtains and watched the moon play shadows with the trees. It was all a dream, an impossible dream, to own a farm. We were realists, we knew the problems; there was no way, in our already frenetic life, that we could accommodate a fruit farm.

It had been a hard-headed, logical, joint decision, taken in our bedroom window the night before, that we did not need it, we could not afford it, we knew nothing of fruit growing, we had too much to do already. We had kissed in the moonlight and gone to bed, having firmly decided that I would not even attend the auction.

Despite this, on the spur of the moment as it were, I had bought it.

I drove home, my mind in a turmoil. Fear chased elation, hope rivalled financial inevitability. I turned into our long drive, pockmarked with holes I had not had time to fill.

Somehow, I didn't notice the untidy garden, already far too big for us to cope with, the tangled expanses of wire netting pens full of ornamental ducks, and the big shed up the back half full of uncompleted incubators. I thought only that we now had a fruit farm.

My wife came out of the kitchen to meet me at the back door. There was that look in her eye.

'Ruth, please,' I said. 'I can explain.'

It sounded a very lame excuse.

'Well?' she said.

'May I come in?' I grinned at her. In spite of her better feelings, I could sense the smile behind her eyes. 'Shall I throw my hat in first?'

The smile broke through. Many, many years ago, lost in the myths of family history, there was an old man very fond of his beer. When, returning from the village pub drunk yet again, he reached his own back door, he would open it gently and throw in his hat. If the hat was promptly thrown out again, it meant his wife was still up, still mad at him, and it was not safe to come in.

If, however, the hat was not thrown back out, his wife had either gone to bed or forgiven him. In either case, it was safe to enter.

The folklore had it that he spent more hours walking up and down outside his house, sobering up, than he did consuming beer.

'You are an idiot,' she said, but she kissed me, and

11

produced the remains of a dried-up lunch, kept warm for several hours past its best eating time.

My hat was not thrown out. We talked, got excited, scared, and dreamed dreams. We had never owned a farm before, not even an apparently little fruit farm. Somehow, we would pay off that vast sum owing to the bank.

Still dreaming, utterly unaware of the enormity of what I had set in motion, I went back to work. Proper work – the surgery and the hospital.

2

Nothing had ever ruffled Mr Allwood senior. His life had been dictated by routine and nothing, but nothing, was allowed to disturb it. Since his retirement many years before, he had acquired an enduring way of life that compensated for the loss of his working office routine.

His one passion was growing begonias, and even they had been brought indoors so that they should be watered exactly at eleven o'clock. The entire backyard of his small terraced house had been turned into a large conservatory to accommodate them.

Order and routine: these were the civilising influences of a man's existence, and had made possible his serene progression to the grand old age of ninety-one.

For seventy-odd years, once he closed his front door behind him, he had been monarch of all he surveyed. He supervised the watering of his begonias at precisely eleven o'clock and had his meals brought to him on a tray at the exactly stipulated time.

During the course of his long and honourable life, he had fathered eleven children, each and every one of them brought up strictly to follow his rules of good order and common decency. Each one, like himself, had been apprenticed, on leaving school, to a respectable calling.

For his own part, many years ago, he had been placed in the Borough Treasurer's Office where, by dint of good attendance and application to his tasks, he had slowly risen to the grand rank of Deputy Borough Treasurer; but he had now been honourably retired for over twenty-five years.

Order and routine had ruled his life, both at home and at work. Naturally, his eldest daughter had not been sent out to work as had all the other children. Her preordained vocation had been to stay at home to help with the demands of such a large family. Her views had not been ascertained – it was assumed to be her moral duty.

As his wife had slowly succumbed to the ever increasing burden and finally died of overwork at an unreasonably early age, this eldest daughter, Laura, stepped into her mother's shoes, and took over the exacting task of the care of her father.

For her, there was never any question of marriage. The essentials of routine and order dictated her future. Her duty was to care for her father, have his meals ready on the appointed hour, and ensure that his begonia watering can was always filled in time for it to equilibrate to room temperature. She had performed her duties in an exemplary manner, until now.

All the old man's sons had done well, but his eldest son, known to everyone as Mister Allwood, the best of all. No one ever called him by his Christian name, it was not fitting for a man of such dignity. The cleverest of an able family, he had stayed at school longer than most, and had then been placed in the office of a large shipyard, where in the fullness of time he had not only risen to become the manager, but had also gained a seat on the board of the company. He had, at one stage, been mayor of the local town.

I had met both him and his eldest sister, Laura, several times, here at the house of begonias, as I came to know it. These begonias were huge, indecent things, with flowers the size of dinner plates – reds, yellows, pinks and creams, all looking as if they had just been made out of crepe paper.

In their pots, they lined the walls, the passages, and every window sill. Each morning, they were all rotated, to ensure that each had its share of sun in the backyard conservatory.

I had discussed the secret of their success with the old man on several occasions. There was no secret, he said, just new compost every spring, and the same corms carefully saved each winter. Every Saturday they had their exact dose of fertiliser, and at eleven o'clock every morning their exact dose of water, at exactly the right temperature.

That particular morning, poor Laura was at virtual breaking point. She was now well past her sixtieth birthday, with grey hair, a face that had never known make-up, and an air of patient submission.

The old man would have been the first to deny that he was in any way autocratic or domineering, and indeed, to the rest of the world he was a mild-mannered, pleasant, old retired public servant. To his daughter he was unconsciously horrible.

I had been summoned, I thought, to attend to his usual, well tended complaint. Like many old folk, the musculature and tone of his stomach had drooped a little with age, so that he suffered from the, to him, acutely embarrassing burping of wind. A predecessor of mine, in the mists of past history, had told him it was all the fault of his gall bladder, and that the cure for such a distressing complaint was a glass of hot water after every meal.

Like his begonias, he was watered with water of exactly the right temperature, at exactly the right time. This ensured the continuity of his serenity, as well as the continued health and beauty of his paper-thin blooms.

That morning, poor Laura had got a little confused. She had poured the kettle of boiling water into the begonia can, and put out a glassful of water with the chill just off it, to stabilise. The first mouthful of lukewarm water had aggravated the old tyrant's discomfort sufficiently to cause him to send out his daughter for his eldest son. The son had summoned me.

Even I could see that something catastrophic had happened to the begonias. Those enormous, multicoloured pastel, paper blooms hung their heads in despair, while the leaves writhed and wilted in agony. They had been watered meticulously with boiling water.

The old man had taken to his bed, preoccupied with his stomach, and was as yet unaware of the plight of his precious begonias.

Laura was shaking and crying. Mr Allwood stood by, outwardly calm.

'Stop it, do,' he said, not unkindly, but impatiently. I felt that he had witnessed similar scenes before.

Laura dabbed at her eyes and twisted the handkerchief with her fingers.

'Whatever made me do it?' she repeated several times. 'However could I have put the boiling water in his can, and the cold water in his glass?'

'Perhaps your mind was on other things,' I suggested.

'No more than usual,' she replied, still twisting the handkerchief, and I noticed for the first time how swollen and arthritic her fingers were.

I also noticed, again for the first time, how unwell generally she looked. Tired, drawn, pale, and as if there had been a recent weight loss. There was a characteristic reddening of the skin across her upper nose, flaring out onto her cheeks: a typical papular butterfly rash.

The last time I had seen such a rash had been in my final exams. I had nearly failed them. Even if I had not known of such a rash before those exams, I certainly knew of it during and after. It had been a very unpleasant half-hour with the dean of the medical school, exposing my ignorance of his favourite subject. Never, not if I lived to be a hundred, could I forget the butterfly rash of Systemic Lupus Erythematosus.

From upstairs a bell rang. Not loud, but insistent, and commanding. Laura stopped crying, visibly pulled herself together, and walked out of the room to answer her father's summons.

After a moment or two, as her footsteps echoed tiredly up the stairs, I made as if to follow her.

'Er,' said Mr Allwood.

16

I turned to him.

'My sister is unwell,' he said carefully. 'I would really like you to see her today. She has resolutely refused to come to see you, on the grounds that you would probably only put her in hospital, and then there would be no one to look after Father.'

I nodded agreement. 'I'll look at him first,' I said, 'and then we'll see Laura afterwards.'

Slowly, and with great dignity, he walked up the stairs. I followed behind and, on reaching the top, was ushered into the small front bedroom.

Mr Allwood senior lay in bed – more, lay in state – while his daughter fussed round him, fluffing his pillows. Deferentially, she backed away for me to move to the bedside.

I smiled at her, noting, as well as that rash, the tired lines on her face, the anaemic pallor, in fact the utter exhaustion of her being, and the gross hot rheumatoid arthritis of her hands. She was indeed severely ill. She coughed, a deep, throaty, bronchitic cough.

'Thank you for coming,' Mr Allwood senior said from his bed, drawing attention back to himself.

He glanced in Laura's direction, with mild but generously forgiving reproach.

'My daughter gave me water of the wrong temperature this morning. It has quite upset my stomach.'

Laura's face went a little paler, and if anything she looked even more tired and exhausted.

'Let me look at it,' I said.

Contentedly, he lay back in the bed, in his rightful place, the centre of attention – a subconscious attitude of mind which was the natural consequence of a lifetime in a household totally subservient to his needs.

'Put out your tongue,' I said. It came out with practised ease, the ease to be expected of one who inspects his tongue regularly for signs of ill health.

It was surprisingly dry, white and scaly, but Mr Allwood

senior had obviously not inspected it himself recently, or he would have drawn my attention to it.

'Put it away,' I said without comment.

His skin, although he was ninety-one, dusky and wrinkled, seemed to me to be somewhat drier that usual, and even less elastic.

I laid a hand on his abdomen. Through the dry, thin skin of old age, I could feel a huge, hard, craggy mass that had not been present the last time I had examined him, some several months ago. It was centred under his right ribs, in his liver, and extended well down into the abdomen.

'That's the spot,' he said as I felt it. 'That's my gall bladder, and where that water has caused the inflammation.'

I was aware of Laura behind me, ill, contrite, guilty and submissive.

I continued the examination. There was the slightest tinge of jaundice in his eyeballs, and small, hard malignant glands palpable in his neck, under his arms and in his groins, in fact, all over his body. They were the deposits of widespread, advanced and inoperable cancer. His pain was due to secondary growth in his liver, pressing on the small bile ducts within it, causing an obstruction and the first stages of jaundice. It had probably been growing slowly and undetected in his aged body for several years, and only now, a matter of months before the end, had it produced signs and symptoms.

His ignorance of his condition was total, and it seemed at that moment unkind to enlighten him, but the nursing burden he would present over the next few months would be much more than his poor daughter could cope with, particularly if she had developed Systemic Lupus Erythematosis.

'Mr Allwood,' I said, feeling the tender area again. He winced. 'You've got a bit of a lump here, that you've not had before.'

18

'I know,' he said. 'It's my gall bladder. I've felt it myself.' He looked down the bed at his daughter. 'Laura knows that water of the wrong temperature will set it off. I have told her many times.'

His eyes were full of reproach – gentle, forgiving, and yet hard, demanding total obedience.

'I think, Mr Allwood, that the water has only drawn our attention to a pre-existing problem,' I said gently. 'You see, that's not just a simple inflammation. It's a deep-seated one. I'm not sure how to treat it. We could do several things, but which one depends on exactly which type of inflammation it is. We need a proper diagnosis.'

I had his full attention. He was aware that I was trying to say, and yet not to say, something.

'I think that we need to do some blood tests, some X-rays, water tests, and so on. I think we had better have you in hospital, get it diagnosed, then we can treat it.'

'There's no need for hospitals,' he said. 'I'm too old for that. At my age, I'm too old for hospitals. Laura can look after me here.'

As far as he was concerned, that was the end of it. He had delivered his verdict. He was not interested in any form of proper diagnosis. He knew it was his gall bladder, aggravated by water of the wrong temperature. We were dismissed. He settled down for a sleep.

Silently we trooped out, down the little flight of stairs, and into the front room.

Laura was extremely apologetic, assuming, like her father, that her mistake with the water was the cause of all the problem.

Gently, I explained to them the true situation.

'The water has got nothing to do with it,' I said. 'He has a cancerous growth, one that has probably arisen from somewhere in his large bowel, that has been quietly and symptomlessly growing for several years. It is only, over the past few months, since it spread to his liver and grew there, that our attention has been drawn to it.'

'Is there anything that can be done?' asked Mr Allwood.

'Not really. At his age, with that degree of spread before it caused symptoms, I think that the main treatment is to keep him comfortable.'

I warned them that his discomfort would get worse, and hot water or cold water would not influence it.

'Is there no chance of an operation, to remove the cancer?' asked Laura.

'None at all, I'm afraid. There's too much of it, scattered all over his body,' I said. 'But I will ask the surgeons to see him. You see, there's a tinge of jaundice already, and as the weeks pass this is going to get worse. There could even be pain, if the bile gets really obstructed.

'If it's bad, it's possible to perform an operation to bypass the obstruction, but this won't alter anything, only make him more comfortable. At the moment it's a wait and see situation. We treat each problem as it arises.'

Laura was very quiet. I looked at her.

'Come next door, with me,' I said to her. 'I want to have a look at this rheumatism of yours.'

Meekly, she came, tending to make light of her symptoms.

I examined her thoroughly. Once the examination was under way, she admitted that the rheumatism was only a small part of her general ill health. That rash was absolutely characteristic. She was distinctly anaemic, had a heart murmur, grossly congested lungs, and numerous rash-like spots over her trunk, as well as a generalised active inflammation of virtually every joint. The whole picture added up to Systemic Lupus Erythematosis.

This rare condition, such a speciality of the Dean of the Medical School, really needed expert assessment. I had not seen, or heard of, a case since the one so painfully experienced in my final exams.

'How long have you been ill?' I asked her quietly, once I had finished.

'Months,' she said simply.

'You know you're very ill, you ought to be in hospital?'
She nodded.

'I can't, though. Not now he's dying of cancer. He needs me.'

'Let me do all the tests,' I said. 'We'll decide after that.'

I wrote out all the necessary forms, gave them to her, and went out into the other room to speak to Mr Allwood, her brother.

'You're quite right,' I told him. 'She is very ill, she ought to be in hospital.'

We agreed to await the results of the tests before making decisions.

Later, when they had all come from the hospital, I showed Fred, our visiting consultant, the results of the investigations I had done. Everything fitted – the white blood cells, the anaemia, the congested chest X-ray.

'She must come in,' said Fred. 'Today. Or you'll be in trouble.'

I explained about the old man.

'Admit him too.' He did not see it as a problem. 'We've got a bed.'

I went round to see Laura and her father, wondering how I could persuade them both to come in.

Mr Allwood answered my knock on the door.

'Thank goodness you've come,' he said, relief in his voice. 'I was just going to phone you. Father's in very severe pain.'

I went upstairs to him. The pain was not really bad, more of a continuous discomfort. It was just that he was unused to unrelieved discomfort. After I had noted his worsening jaundice and felt his hard, tender lump, I suggested hospital again. He declined the offer.

'Have you told him about Laura?' I asked his son, when I was back downstairs.

'No,' he said.

21

The bell rang again. Gentle, demanding, assuming instant response.

'Where is Laura?' I asked.

'She's in bed, too,' he replied. 'She's not well at all.'

The bell rang again, this time a little louder, a little longer.

We looked at each other. 'He's got a very nasty temper when he's crossed,' said Mr Allwood. 'He doesn't show it often, but when he does, it's fearsome.'

The bell rang again. Insistent, almost angry.

'I'll go and see him again,' I said. 'and Laura at the same time.'

Slowly, with the bell still ringing, I walked back up the stairs and onto the little landing. Laura, weak, pale, and with obvious pain in her feet, was edging herself along the passage wall from her bedroom.

She looked awful, as if she was about to faint. Her hair, matted and uncombed, hung about her head. She was still in her crumpled and sweaty white cotton nightdress. She swayed, as if she was about to fall over.

I caught hold of her arm.

'You'd better get back to bed,' I said.

'But Father ... He's ringing his bell.'

I led her back the few steps to her bedroom, still protesting. She lay back on the bed, feverish and exhausted.

'I'll see to him,' I said.

The bell was now loud, and forceful. I walked back into the old man's bedroom. There was no sign of Mr Allwood, his son.

'Where's Laura?' the old man demanded, in a surprisingly strong voice. 'I have rung my bell.'

'She's ill in bed,' I replied. 'So ill, in fact, I'm going to take her into hospital, now, this morning.'

'She is not ill,' he stated. 'She's been like this before. It is past the time for my coffee. She has not brought it.'

'I have told you,' I said, 'she is ill in bed, and is not going to bring your coffee ... '

'I tell you she is,' he interrupted. His eyes blazed. Old and weak as he was, he clutched the handle of that bell so that the knuckles turned white. He shook it at me. His jaundiced eyes fixed themselves on me, coldly, angrily.

'Send Laura to me, now,' he said.

'I'm sorry,' I said, and turned to leave the room. I could hear Mr Allwood coming up the stairs. He came into the room, bearing the old man's coffee.

'Where's Laura?' his father snapped at him.

'She's in bed,' I told him again. 'In about an hour, the ambulance will come to take her into hospital. She is gravely ill.'

'Nonsense. I do not believe in hospitals. Her place is here, to look after me. I forbid it.'

I walked out of the room, along the passage to Laura. She had heard every word, and was silently weeping.

'I've let him down,' she said. 'Now, after all this time, when he's ill and dying, I've let him down.'

'Not your fault,' I said, feeling somewhat inadequate in this situation. 'We can't be ill to order, and you're no use as you are. Got to get you better first.'

Raised words were still coming from the other bedroom as I left, to organise the ambulance. The dignified, successful business man was being reduced to the status of a schoolboy, with angry, scathing words. He was as much in awe of his father as his poor sister was.

In hospital, Laura did not respond well. She was unhappy, guilty that she had deserted her father. Despite large doses of steroids and antibiotics, the infective process in her lungs progressed to frank pneumonia. I agreed with Fred that she should be transferred to Norwich, to the intensive care unit.

Mr Allwood senior fared no better. He was very demanding. The flash of temper had gone, and he went back to his reproachful correction of the rest of his family's efforts. Nothing they did was right, but they all obeyed his every whim, as he made plain was only right and proper. I told him that Laura was gravely ill, and might possibly not come out of hospital. Solemnly he nodded his head, indicating with every movement that Laura had committed an unforgivable sin by not being present when he was ill. He did not spontaneously enquire after her.

Slowly, inexorably, his jaundice deepened, his pain increased. Fred and the surgeon came out to see him. We all agreed that a palliative operation to relieve his jaundice was not now indicated, it was too late; the surgery would only hasten his end.

At this point, he stated that he was now ready to go into hospital, to have that operation. We had to tell him, as kindly as we could, that there was now no point. He made it plain, that if only Laura had not left him alone at the critical time, he would have had the operation before and so saved himself all this needless suffering, and the rest of the family the necessity of doing Laura's job.

His accusations were so gentle, so believable, his air of long-suffering, injured dignity so plausible, that had I not known the truth I, too, would have accused Laura of unkind neglect.

Unfortunately, his unhappy recriminations were relayed to her, increasing her guilt, a guilt that was aggravated when he finally slipped away one night. She was still too ill to come, and she was still too ill in Norwich to attend his funeral.

Eventually, she recovered enough to leave hospital. Mr Allwood brought her home.

The house was exactly as she had left it, except that her father was no longer there. At first the family came to see her fairly regularly, but once they had established that she was well enough to walk about, the frequency of their visits dropped off.

They had been accustomed to visiting the old man, and now that he was dead, there was no need. Quietly, Laura settled into a life of solitary routine.

24

Nothing changed in the house. The begonias were repotted and fertilised, each placed in its proper place. The old man's bedroom was cleaned, and his bed made as if he would be sleeping in it that night. Even the bell beside the bed was regularly polished, and placed exactly where he could still reach it. The whole house became a shrine to his memory, with the begonias the memorial flowers.

Laura, her disease barely arrested and controlled, struggled to maintain the house.

'Order and discipline. That's what he liked,' she said. 'We must keep up the standards.'

I let it be known that I should like to see Mr Allwood, as I was worried about his sister's behaviour.

We met, in the front room, surrounded by prize begonias. Ceremonially we admired them.

Laura brought in some coffee, two cups not three. She started offering sugar and biscuits. Mr Allwood gave her a gentle, but firm look.

'Stop fussing, do.'

He was an exact copy of his father. Laura went back to the kitchen, as the look he gave her told her to.

The future was mapped as plain as plain. There was nothing I could do to alter it. It was all ordered and routine.

3

I surveyed our garden with increasing despair. The work involved was just too much. The small patches cleared after hours and hours of back-breaking toil, weeding and trimming and hoeing, only succeeded in showing up just how much remained to be done. In the years that we had owned it, much had been accomplished to lessen the work involved, but all these alterations were yet more work in themselves – there seemed no end to it. And now we had bought a fruit farm. Even if we did have the time to spend pulling weeds out of a herbaceous border, it was not an occupation that either Ruth or I really enjoyed. She in particular was not a natural gardener: one day's frenzied efforts produced two more days of tidying up, usually done by me weeks later.

In its prime, our garden had been a showcase of summer colour. A succession of previous owners had been what Ruth's splendid old grandmother would have dismissed derisively as 'Tuppenny packet of seed people'.

The whole of the front and side gardens, nearly two acres in all, had been devoted to multiple many-sided beds of gaudy annuals. Salvias had been the favourite – six thousand of them, it was boasted – and all grown at home by two full-time gardeners. They might have liked lawns patterned with stars and crescents and squares, all filled with massed, brilliant red, all neatly edged with blue and white, and requiring the services of two full-time skilled men, but those days were gone.

The two full-time gardeners were now me, alone, and I was busy doing something else. My gardening philosophy was simple: if I couldn't mow it, I mowed round it. I could race round the garden on a mower with a three-foot cut once a week, and render the whole thing neat and tidy. That which I couldn't mow, grew in profusion. The main problem with my sort of gardening was mole-hills, clogging and breaking my mower as I hit them at speed.

Great strides in sorting out our garden into a more manageable shape had originally been made by a splendid itinerant known as Gypsy Smith. Though obviously not his real name, it was the one he was known by and the only one to put in his record cards. There were no permanent record cards either; his medical history was contained in a massive pile of temporary resident forms lost somewhere in the cupboards of the Ministry of Health. They, like himself, had no fixed abode, being shuttled from temporary shelf to temporary doctor, as he travelled round the country. The whole lot usually arrived in a huge parcel some nine months after Gypsy had moved on.

Together with the medical record forms was a heap of letters, of almost equal volume, from the Social Security people and various Regional Medical Officers of Health, all asking for confirmation of his existence, and demanding proof of his entitlement to sick pay. Our little area had a newly appointed RMO who, in his short career as a general practitioner, had once been consulted by Gypsy Smith. Neither had been impressed by the other. The doctor had pronounced Gypsy to be a malingerer, a parasite on society, and had forcefully told him so. Gypsy had declared the other to be an ignorant fool. Blows had been struck.

With that exception, the information on every temporary resident form was virtually identical. It was recorded that he was a known gastric ulcer sufferer, that he had had two unsuccessful operations, and now took gallons of a proprietary indigestion mixture. They also stated that, between periods of complete normality, he developed bouts of severe, incapacitating abdominal pain. During these bouts he needed a certificate for his sick pay. Most of the

27

doctors consulted, though formally expressing doubts as to the presence and severity of his pain, had erred on the side of giving him another medical certificate.

I had known him on and off, as he came and went, for many years. His method of apparently milking the system was perfect. There was absolutely no way of proving or disproving the account of his pain without hospital investigations.

Regional Medical Officers of Health all over the country wished formally to examine him, and had sent out innumerable letters of appointment for this to be done. Any mention of hospitals or RMO examinations caused Gypsy to move reluctantly on and seek the advice of a more sympathetic doctor. About four weeks in any one place appeared to be the average length of stay, and he seldom sought the advice of any individual doctor more than once.

* * *

I appeared to be one of the exceptions. The trouble was that I believed him. The scars on his abdomen were genuine enough, and without any doubt he did suffer bouts of severe pain at very frequent intervals. The only problem was that, between these bouts, he felt no obligation to terminate, however temporarily, his one sure source of income.

I had given my opinion as to his state of health on one of the many enquiry forms that had actually arrived while Gypsy was still in the area. Our previous RMO, with only a few months to go before his retirement, had not formally disagreed. He had allowed Gypsy to continue to draw benefits during the remainder of his tenure of office.

The new RMO had decided views of his own. These, of course, were influenced by his first-hand experience. As far as he was concerned, his opinion of Gypsy as a malingerer and parasite on the state still stood. He was determined to track him down and eliminate him from the system.

28

Gypsy, meanwhile, carried on as normal. For most of the time, he was many miles away and well out of the area of our new and zealous RMO. In terms of work, he could turn his hand to anything and, depending on the weather, his state of mind, and the rate of pay, wandered from fruit picking, to tarmac laying, to labouring on a building site. He was part of a close-knit, itinerant gang. The gang were in the area at this time, moving earth on the new town by-pass road works. They had a couple of battered old lorries, several wheel barrows, and a shovel apiece.

Gypsy had come into the surgery late one evening, just as I was about to go home. There was no doubt that, on this occasion, his pain was genuine and somewhat severe. All he wanted from me was the usual prescription for his massive doses of indigestion mixture.

I enquired if he needed a further certificate.

'No thanks,' he replied. 'The one I've got is good for a few weeks yet.'

We discussed his ulcer for several minutes. 'Really, you know,' I said, 'you ought to go into hospital, get some X-rays done, and get that stomach of yours really sorted out. The sort of life you're leading isn't doing it any good – irregular meals, too much beer and so on.'

'Hospitals. No thanks,' he said. 'I've been in twice, had an operation each time.'

He looked hard back across the desk at me. 'Don't know if you've ever had an operation, Doc, but it damn well hurts. Far worse than any pain I get now. And do you know, neither of them has made the slightest bit of difference. The only difference it's made is to make my stomach smaller. Can't damn well eat anything much at all now.'

He looked down at the desk, and then back up at me. 'That mixture, that helps, as long as I drink enough of it.'

'You ought not to work and draw sick pay,' I said quietly. 'For one thing, they'll catch up with you, and for the other, you ought to be resting. Working and worrying only make it worse.'

'It's difficult,' he replied, after a moment. 'You see, the gang, the boys, they are the only home and family I've got. I've got to pull my weight, can't live on their money all the time. When I can work, I can earn money. When the pain's bad, I'm no good for anything. I need that sick pay just to survive.'

We agreed that he should come back after a couple of weeks. Casually, I asked him what was happening to all the earth that was being moved.

'Oh, we're dumping it,' he replied.

I thought of all those geometrical flowerbeds and wondered aloud how much earth would be needed to fill them in up to lawn level.

'Only a load or two,' he answered, and then offered to have a look next time he was passing with a load of soil.

He returned, as arranged, when he had need of more medicine, and another certificate.

'How is the pain?' I asked him as he lay on the couch.

'Much the same,' he said. 'Some days it's really bad, others I don't notice it.'

He sat up after I had prodded his stomach. There was without doubt still the residual tenderness of a chronic ulcer. I gave him another prescription, and a further certificate for another month's sick pay.

'We're all lined up to do your garden next week,' he announced, as he did up his trousers. 'The boys are between jobs now, and we'll get it done before we move on.'

'But what about that certificate?' I protested, pointing to it on the desk. 'I can't sign you on as not fit for work, and employ you at the same time.'

'Oh, I won't be working,' he said sincerely. 'I'll just be around to see that the boys put it in the right place.'

He walked to the door. 'See you next week,' he said, as he closed it behind him.

It was much less than a week later when, coming home to lunch one morning, my mind miles away on other things, half-way up the drive I nearly ran into the back of a parked lorry, laden with turf. Beside it was an enormous heap of soil, and skilfully shovelling the soil into a wheelbarrow was Gypsy Smith.

He waved at me, then continued shovelling. The heap of soil completely blocked the drive. I switched off the engine, got out of the car, and watched him wheel his heavy barrow across the lawn. Several of the beds were already filled in and covered with fresh turf. There was only one other man spreading the soil as Gypsy brought it to him. There was no sign of the rest of the gang.

'I thought you said you wouldn't be working,' I said.

For a fleeting moment he almost looked embarrassed. 'Ah, well,' he said. 'I'm not really, just keeping an eye, making sure things get done.'

He tipped out the soil onto a fresh crescent bed and went back for another load. His mate spread it expertly, stamped it down and covered it with turf. He grunted a greeting at me, but did not speak.

By evening, the sweep of green lawn, uninterrupted to the road, looked impressive. Ruth and I stood and admired it.

'It looks good,' I said to Gypsy.

'Better still when we've finished,' he answered. His dislike of fiddling little beds seemed greater than mine. It was a joy to see them barrow in the soil, then cut the turf to fit and roll it flat, so that within a few days it was difficult to tell where all those fiddly little beds had been.

'Just wants finishing off along the road,' Gypsy remarked. 'It needs a nice shrub border along there.'

I agreed. The original hedge providing privacy from the road had been uprooted some years previously, in an attempt to make the garden modern, trendy, and open-plan. Only a low wall now marked the boundary, so that all those passing by could see the glory of the salvias of the philistine.

31

Gypsy and his friend soon altered that. Digging side by side, and shaping the edges as the fancy took them, they scalloped and made that front border.

We agreed that it now needed filling with shrubs.

'You can get all you want, cheap, at Wisbech auctions,' Gypsy told us; so the following Saturday, squeezed into the cab of his decrepit old lorry, we made the trip.

Gypsy drove, and although he said nothing, it was plain that he was in considerable discomfort.

I wandered in amazement through the acres and acres of plants, all laid out for sale. The auctioneer started, and moved swiftly down the rows. He asked a price, there was a nod, perhaps another, and as quickly as that, the lots were sold. Several times I thought I would bid, but by the time I was organised to do so, it was too late.

After hurried consultations with Gypsy, with him bidding on my behalf, we rapidly accumulated more than a decent lorry-load of assorted, utterly unknown to me, species of shrubs.

In triumph we bore them home, sorted them out into what we hoped were the right sizes and colours and positions, and, by Sunday evening, the lot had been planted in our new border.

We thanked Gypsy for his help, paid him, and watched him climb painfully up into his cab.

'You must get something done about that stomach,' I said. 'You're not really fit for work, are you?'

Reluctantly, and distinctly uneasy, I watched his lorry drive away.

In the post on Monday morning was a letter from the newly appointed Regional Medical Officer of Health, demanding to know why I had issued a certificate to one Gypsy Smith, in the face of his most recent circular, commanding any doctor seeing him, not to do so.

The reason was quite simple: I had not seen the circular. Such things were addressed to Mac, my dour Scottish senior partner, and he had never bothered to pass it on.

I showed my letter to Mac, and told him about Gypsy and the gardening.

'What do I do now?' I asked him.

'Nothing,' he said dismissively. 'Ignore the pompous little tit.'

Mac had a very low opinion of him: they had apparently known each other for a long time. I had only met him once, when he had come out to inspect our drug books, and he had not impressed me either. He took his duties of checking on our certificates very seriously. So far, apart from this, he had not disagreed with any of mine.

I filed the letter with the latest temporary resident form for Gypsy Smith.

A few weeks passed by. Another letter from the RMO informed me that Gypsy had not kept his appointment to be medically examined, and demanded my comments.

Neither Mac nor I had any, so we filed it with the first. The letter also pointed out that my last certificate had now expired, and under no circumstances were any further certificates to be issued, as the man was obviously a malingerer and had no further right to be a drain on the state.

Since Gypsy did not come to see me, I presumed that he had moved on again. He was not at the front of my thoughts when I picked up the telephone to answer it.

'It's the coroner's officer here,' said the voice. 'Bedford Police. A man by the name of Gypsy Smith has been brought in to casualty, dead. The relatives say that you are his doctor: can you issue a death certificate?'

I sat in my chair. 'No,' I said weakly. I couldn't really take it in. 'He had a chronic gastric ulcer,' I said at last. 'What happened?'

'According to this statement here,' replied the policeman, 'he was in perpetual pain. It got very bad last night, so bad his friends wanted to get help, but he wouldn't let them. Didn't believe in hospitals, apparently. They brought him in on the back of a lorry this morning, and he died soon after.'

'His ulcer must have perforated, then,' I said. 'At least, I presume that's what happened.'

'Could you issue a death certificate to that effect, then?' he asked again. 'It would save a lot of bother here.'

'Not really,' I said. 'I haven't seen him in the last two weeks, so legally I can't, and in any case, if it had happened here, I should still have asked for a coroner's post mortem.'

He agreed to send me the results of the examination when it had been done. Poor old Gypsy, I thought. It was such a short while ago that he was so full of life planting shrubs in my garden. Some considerable time later, I rang the bell for the next patient.

After a few days, the Bedford policeman was as good as his word, and sent me a copy of the post mortem report. Gypsy had indeed had a massive gastric ulcer, a recurrence in the remnant of his stomach after all that surgery. This had perforated, causing considerable bleeding. Death was due to natural causes. There would be no inquest.

In the same post was a further demand from the RMO on the current state of health of Gypsy Smith, with a rather curt handwritten note demanding a reply to his previous communication.

I pinned the post mortem report to it and returned the form to sender, without comment. It was a long time before we had any further correspondence from him, of any nature.

At first the garden had all looked very neat and tidy, as the plants grew and came into flower. Gypsy had done a good job with his digging, but as the seasons had come and gone, so had our shrub bed reverted to nature.

Now, for want of a hoe, the weeds had grown taller than the shrubs, the grass had grown taller than the mower could cope with, and it was all desperately in need of a tidy up. But other things really did have priority.

At first, with memories of Gypsy, we had tried spasmodically to help keep it tidy, but it was a losing battle: each year the weeds grew stronger. It was about three years since we had seen him, and there seemed no prospect of help in sight.

* * *

The old boy walked slowly up the drive, pushing his bicycle. Tied to the crossbar was a spade that looked as old as he was, worn and polished with use. He was dressed in his standard uniform of blue apron overalls, dark waistcoat and jacket. The legs of his trousers were held tightly to the top of his boots with cycle clips. He could have been any age between sixty-five and ninety.

'Your garden looks in a mess,' he said.

'Yes,' was all I could reply. It certainly was in a mess. The old boy stared at it. I looked at all those weeds, flourishing over the top of Gypsy's shrubs.

'It needs digging,' he said.

'Yes,' I agreed. 'It does.'

He continued to look at it. 'I charge fifty pence an hour.'

That seemed reasonable to me.

'Going to take a fair while,' he said evenly.

I agreed. There was a lot of work.

'I've brought my spade, he said. 'May as well make a start now.' Unhurriedly, he walked down the garden to the end of the front border, and began to dig. The rhythm of his digging was slow, even, and methodical, such a contrast to Gypsy's. Gypsy's digging was like mine, frenetic activity between periods of exhaustion.

Methodically the old man dug his way all round the garden. It took him several weeks. I had assumed that, when he had completed his task, he would ask for payment, and further instructions. He did neither. Like the man painting the Forth Bridge, he just dug it all over again.

Little rituals imperceptibly developed, like morning coffee and after-lunch tea. If it was raining, he didn't come.

35

About once a month Ruth enquired delicately how much we owed him.

'I expect it's a few pounds by now,' was the ritual reply, and although he never actually came straight out with a sum of money, somehow, discreetly, the exact amount changed hands with enormous dignity.

He became as much a part of the garden as the shrubs in it.

His name was Walter George Lambert. His father had also been named Walter George Lambert, and to distinguish him from his father in his youth, he had invariably been called 'The Boy Walter'. The name persisted, as his father had lived, active and alert, till almost ninety.

The Boy Walter's eldest son, himself now almost a pensioner in his own right, also christened Walter George Lambert, answered to the name of 'Young Walter'. Young Walter was summoned for all the heavy work.

'The Boy will give me a hand with that,' we would be informed. We never paid 'The Boy'. All remuneration was via his father. Like the village, we soon grew to know them as 'The Old Boy' and 'The Young Boy'

The Old Boy was treated by the children with enormous respect. He was to them at all times 'Mr Lambert'. The place where all the garden tools were kept was Mr Lambert's shed. The only tools that he ever used were his own spade, and his own reap hook for cutting long grass. They hung on their own special nails, and were sacred; somehow they would have been defiled if anyone else had used them. Even the children felt this, and naturally gave them the same respect that they gave their owner.

Alongside his spade hung his mole traps. It was a never-ending job trapping moles in our garden. Mole-hills seemed to me to illustrate the contrariness of the principles of existence. One went to enormous trouble to create a garden, to plant it just so, to mow the lawn to perfection, to trim the edges, to get it right; and then, just as all the work seemed to be done, and one could really sit down to admire it, a family of moles would move in, tunnel under the flowers, uprooting and killing them, and pile heaps of earth all over the lawn, totally ruining it with their shallow tunnels. Life was just like that: as soon as everything seemed to be right, the moles of adversity would tunnel haphazardly through it, covering it with base earth and breaking the dreams, as they passed uncaringly by.

To me, moles were vandals, mindlessly destroying the peace and harmony of my home, in their greedy, blind, underground search for worms, utterly unaware of the importance of my higher feelings above their base struggle for existence.

I waged war on them too, down on the island. The earth underneath a duck's nest is warm and moist, as the vegetation quietly rots and ferments. Here, where the living is good, the worms tend to congregate, and are avidly sought out by the moles. No duck can incubate with equanimity when being undermined by an erupting mole-hill. We were losing far too many nests to the moles, nests which had a hard commercial value.

The afternoon round of the mole traps became almost as much of a ritual as that of morning coffee. Mr Lambert had taken on our eldest son John as a molecratching apprentice. He would rush out to join him as soon as he returned from school.

On the day that I had bought the fruit farm, the two of them were deep in conversation under the lime tree.

I walked quietly up to them. Neither of them knew what I had done, and I was bursting to tell them.

'Now this here's the main run,' The Old Boy was explaining as he demonstrated. With a few careful sweeps of his gnarled old hand, he brushed aside the newly erupted mole-hill.

'Now, in the middle here, you'll find the hole.'

He probed gently till he found it, and, working round

with his finger, delicately removed the loose earth and exposed the entrance to the tunnel.

We both peered down into it.

'Put your hand in, very carefully,' The Old Boy said to John. 'Can you feel the two tunnels – this one coming up from over here, and that one going back down away over this side?'

John agreed that he could indeed feel the two tunnels. The Old Boy showed him how to carefully remove the soil between the two ends of the tunnels, so that there was just room to place in the trap. Whichever tunnel the mole came up, he would have to pass through the centre of the trap in order to continue into the other run, and so trigger its vice-like jaws.

The trap, having been delicately set and placed in the hole, was carefully covered with long grass and soil to keep out the light.

'About every four hours, that old mole runs,' he said. He paused, and looked at his watch. 'In about another hour, I think you'll find him in there.'

He straightened up from his trap, and looked enquiringly at me.

'I've bought the fruit farm,' I said.

He looked down at me, and then at his boots.

'Have you really?' said John, interrupting. 'Does Mummy know yet?'

'Yes,' I said. 'I told her at lunchtime.'

'Was she mad?' he asked, in a matter-of-fact tone, presuming that naturally she would be.

'Yes she was,' I said.

The Old Boy smiled.

'Do you want to come and look at it?'

Together the three of us walked over the road. The Old Boy kicked the rock-hard clods of the ploughed field, scraped the earth with his toes between the strawberries, and walked silently through all those rows of apple trees.

There was so much to explore: it was far bigger than I had ever anticipated. We completed the circle round it, and returned home.

'What do you think of it?' I asked anxiously.

The Old Boy kicked a piece of soil.

'That's poison starved,' he said. 'Poison starved.'

'How, what do you mean?' I said, somewhat taken aback.

'Too many years of trees,' he said quietly. 'Too much fertiliser out of a bag. Too much irrigation water. Too many weedkillers. The nature of the soil's gone.'

He looked at me squarely. 'I tell you, it's poison starved. Take years to put it right.'

I could feel that family of moles burrowing under the lawn of my life.

We walked up the drive, past the old lime tree. John walked over to where they had set their trap. As he approached, the trap clicked and jumped. He pull it out in triumph, a freshly dead mole firmly held in its jaws. One less to plague me.

The Old Boy looked at his watch. 'Dead on time,' he said.

'Can we put that soil straight?' I asked.

'Oh yes,' he said. 'Just takes a little while, and a lot of muck.'

John carefully reset his mole trap. I was resetting the mole traps of my life, too.

4

Manure was on my mind. Horse manure, pig manure, cow manure – any variety of animal excreta would do; the problem was, there didn't seem to be any around. The Old Boy was right. Whichever way I looked at it, that farm was short of it.

Muck, The Old Boy called it. Sir Percival, the man who was selling the farm to me, was more delicate: he called it organic fertiliser and soil conditioner. He agreed that the farm was in great need of it. During all his years of ownership, there had never been any money to buy any, or indeed any other local farmer with any to spare. He informed me it was like gold dust, about as plentiful, and more expensive.

After the sale, some little time passed before we actually took possession. Acutely conscious that the land was 'poison starved', Ruth and I had accepted Sir Percy's invitation to go round a farm walk with him, and meet the staff.

Unknown to me at the time of the sale, the solicitor handling the whole process for me had put in a bid, stating that we would take all the machinery at valuation, and keep on all the staff.

I had discovered, later, that the staff consisted of the gouty Sir Percy himself, his nephew, who had decided that he could make a better living selling insurance, and three men.

I knew that the nephew had already gone. Sir Percival would stay till Michaelmas, and then formally hand over. After our official walk round, we were to meet the men.

I was very apprehensive. What I knew about fruit growing could not only have been written on the back of the proverbial postage stamp, but also it would not have needed a very large stamp.

The staff were agricultural workers, with a lifetime on the land, most of it growing fruit. I felt very ignorant and inadequate, as Sir Percy walked round, pointing out the various good and bad features of the place, dashing off the names of fiendish-sounding chemical sprays, without which pest and disease would claim the entire crop, and exhorting me not to forget to do this and that in its due season. There was so much of it, coming so fast, that the vast majority of his advice went over my head.

I would have been much happier discussing his gout, but he never as much as mentioned it. Since I had explained the scientific basis of his treatment, he had taken his pills exactly as prescribed, and had had no further attacks of pain.

We came eventually to the apple orchard, where the crop of fruit had all been picked and sold, and where the men were reputed to be working, cleaning up, and making a start on the winter pruning.

'By the way,' said Sir Percy, as we walked into the middle of it. Four acres of trees seemed an awful lot of trees to prune, one at a time. I looked up and down the rows, and could only see one man, small and insignificant in the distance, working in the middle of a tree.

'You'll be a bit short staffed, to start with,' said Sir Percy as we walked towards the solitary figure.

'Oh,' I said. 'Why's that?'

There was a slightly embarrassed pause.

'Well, you see, they all knew I was packing up. The only person who had shown the slightest interest in buying the land, before you decided to, was that speculative builder. They knew they wouldn't have a job with him, they've sort of made other arrangements. Two of them left last week.'

'I see,' I said, not knowing whether to be relieved that the wage bill would be so drastically reduced, or anxious that the necessary work would not be done. I didn't even know how much was involved.

'Er,' he paused. I could see that he was now definitely embarrassed. 'Frank,' nodding his head in the direction of the solitary man still pruning his tree, 'has been with me, and my mother before me, for over fifty years. He came to work for her when he was eleven, as boots boy, and has been here ever since. This farm is a part of him, he's been a sort of foreman most of my life. The land really is his in his mind. He planted all these trees thirty years ago.'

I looked down the row. Frank had finished that tree, and moved to another. He had either not seen us, or deemed us none of his business.

'He's very worried that you are a doctor, and know nothing about fruit. He could retire, and draw his old age pension, but he's half scared of what you are going to do to his trees in his absence, and half anxious to go.'

Sir Percy stopped walking, and turned to face me. 'He says he's going to meet you today, and depending on how you square up, will let me know whether he's staying or going.'

'As bad as that?' I said, half-laughing.

Ruth gave a wan smile. 'What are we going to do, if he does leave?'

I shook my head. There was no answer. The enormity of what we had done in buying the place suddenly hit me.

Slowly, in silence, we approached Frank. He continued unconcernedly to prune his tree. Fairly large branches fell about his feet.

'Frank,' said Sir Percy, 'meet Dr and Mrs Jackson.'

Ruth was nearest to him. She held out her hand and gave him a warm smile.

'I'm glad to meet you,' she said. 'Have your ears burned while we were walking down? Sir Percival's been telling us all about you – how essential you are in running the place, how you planted all these trees.'

Frank did not speak. A shy smile appeared momentarily on his face, and his ears reddened a little. He was a round, shortish man, with an egg-shaped head. His whole body seemed to speak. One was aware that Frank was not displeased, but it was difficult to say why.

'Hallo,' I said holding out my hand. He shook it awkwardly; his vibrations said he was not used to shaking hands with doctors.

I jumped in with both feet.

'Sir Percy tells me you've agreed to stay on, and help us run the place,' I said.

His vibes did not disagree.

'You know we know nothing about fruit,' I continued. 'We've got a lot to learn.'

'Yes,' he said quietly, in a soft Suffolk voice. 'There'll be a lot to get done before Christmas.'

Thus it was agreed that he would stay on and teach us about fruit growing.

Once Michaelmas was past, and the farm, and the enormous bank loan that went with it, were ours, I raised again the subject of manure with Frank.

He did not disagree. 'Wouldn't do any harm,' he said. 'The trees are all right.'

He thought for a minute. The vibes were incredibly neutral, there was no great reaction.

He said in that soft voice of his, 'It's where they've been pulled out the land's bad. The subsoil has been pulled to the top, there's no structure, no life.' I had his permission to acquire some muck.

I started asking round all my farmer patients, eyeing covetously the slurry behind their cowsheds, the middens in their yards, and the enormous sheds full of fattening cattle, up to their axles in all that glorious muck.

The word of my need spread rapidly. For the same reason that I needed it, so did they. It was incredible the speed with which they closed ranks, raised their eyes to heaven, and priced themselves out of the market.

Past medical favours, promises of special treatment to

43

come, were to no avail. Their need was greater than mine. Muck was the life blood of any farm; only a fool sold his life blood.

I cornered Old George in his pigsty. He was shovelling mountains of the lovely stuff into his great barrow. There was an incredibly large heap of it outside his sheds, by the side of his greenhouses. The fermenting juices from it ran into the ditch and away across to the marsh. Tactfully, I hinted that it might be for sale. Delicately, I thought, I asked about the arthritis of his hips, and if he had enough Butazolidine pills.

With enormous dignity, he stopped, wiped his hands on his trousers, and produced his tobacco tin.

Carefully he charged a piece of cigarette paper with a pinch from his tin, smoothing it level with a horny finger. Slowly, delicately, he rolled it, raised it to his mouth, licked the gummed edge, placed the resultant cigarette between his lips, and then patted his pockets for the matches.

He struck first one match, then another, and finally a third, before his cigarette burned to his satisfaction.

Slowly he shook his head.

'Sorry, Doc. Can't let any of that go. Place would be nothing without it.'

Somehow, subtly, our relationship had changed with my request and his refusal. He did not ask for more pills, and I walked sadly away.

If even George wouldn't let me have any, I should have to devise some other way of rejuvenating the soil, just as Sir Percy had done.

My next visit that afternoon was to the Boar. The Boar, chairman of the parish council, self-categorised as emperor of the village, had been slowly dying of a cancer of the prostate for several years. He was only kept alive by his feud with Old George.

George had wanted to build houses on one of his fields. The Boar had publicly stated that it would be done over his dead body. Somehow, with the Boar's illness, they had compromised, and just one small part had been sold off, and a short cul-de-sac of closely spaced, identical little bungalows erected.

The Boar had tended to lose heart again, when George had named the street 'Boresboddy Close'.

He was now fading away. He had not got long to live. His wife had accepted it, and it would be a relief to everyone, not least the Boar, when the time finally came.

I knocked on the front door.

Mrs Boar had never liked me, but over the years had come to accept me as a necessary evil. I was one of the few people who knew that under the commodious wig she always wore was not hair, but a mass of large, ugly red lumps, turban tumours. The only other person, to my knowledge, who was aware of their existence was Old George. She was acutely embarrassed by them, they had blighted her life.

The medical profession was unable to do anything about them, in fact had made them worse with unhelpful surgery and X-rays. I was the embodiment of all the uselessness of doctors everywhere.

Strangely, she had accepted her husband's cancer and, in her own way, had been grateful for the treatment that had extended his life for these few extra years.

She opened the door to my knock. Old George had once described her as a vulture in a frilly hat. I was struck by the aptness of that description.

Her face was gaunt, haggard, tired, and despair was written all over it. Her small eyes, either side of that huge beaklike nose, were moist, and almost shut. I knew before she spoke.

'He's dead, God rest him.' Her voice, which could normally shatter glass, was flat and tired.

'When?' I asked.

'Just now. Just before you knocked.'

45

'Put the kettle on,' I said. 'I'll go and see him and join you in the kitchen.'

I walked through into what had been the dining-room, before they had moved his bed downstairs.

Pale and wasted, the Boar lay dead. She had already straightened his limbs, and pulled the sheet up over his head.

It was sad to see him so. In life and health he had been fat, bombastic, always sure of the rightness of his cause. Slowly, I pulled the sheet back up over his face. The village would not be the same without him.

I went through to the kitchen, and shared a silent cup of tea with Mrs Boar. It was the first she had ever made for me. Peace, a truce, was in the silence.

I wrote out the death certificate, and gave it to her.

'You'll be all right?' I asked. 'Alone?'

She nodded.

Quietly, I walked away.

A week later, on a cold, wet, rainy morning, to my intense surprise, Old George walked into the surgery. His clothes were soaking wet, the rain still dripping off his hair. He looked very uncomfortable.

As a matter of principle, he never came to the surgery, always asked for a visit or a repeat prescription. The receptionist was always happy for him not to come, for, equally on principle, he came directly from his pigs, boots and all.

'Come in,' I said, as he hobbled painfully across the room. He was bent nearly double, and obviously in considerable pain.

I pointed to the chair. 'Sit down.'

There was only the faintest aroma of pigs about him. Though wet, he wore a clean shirt, with collar and tie, a smart blue suit, and shiny black shoes.

I suddenly realised that the tie he was wearing was black.

'You've been to the Boar's funeral, then?' I said.

'Aye. Poor old sod.'

He hobbled to the chair and tried to sit, but couldn't make it. The combination of his stiff, rigid hip joints, and the acute back pain that he was in, left him hanging painfully over the chair.

I helped him up, and over to the examination couch. He left wet footprints all over the floor. Painfully, he managed to lie down.

'What happened?' I asked. 'They didn't ask you to be one of the pall bearers, did they?'

Painfully he shook his head, and smiled. Drips fell off his hair onto the pillow.

'All this damn rain,' he said. 'It made the graveside very muddy.'

A spasm of pain made him wince. He tried to move, and winced again.

'They'd put boards round the grave, and covered them with that green sacking stuff. They were very slippery.'

He winced again, and I thought about giving him a pain-killing injection.

'They lowered the old sod into the grave all right.' He paused, trying to get into a more comfortable position. 'They left a lot of mud on the sacking.'

He paused again, and then a cackle of laughter broke through his pain. It hurt his back, and he stopped.

'Mrs Boar,' he laughed, and winced simultaneously, 'Mrs Boar came up to throw a handful of soil into the grave. She slipped, and bloody nearly fell in with him.'

There were tears in his eyes, whether from laughter or pain I couldn't tell.

'Go on,' I said.

'Feet first,' he said. 'Feet first, she went in. Shot in like a . . . ' He stopped, the tears were caused by pain. It took a moment to regain his composure.

He started to speak again, but he was serious now.

'That wig she wears. It started to come off as she fell. I couldn't stand by and let that happen, not at her husband's funeral, poor old sod.'

47

'What happened then?'

'I had to catch her, didn't I?'

'Did she fall in the grave?' He shook his head. 'Had to catch her, didn't I?' he repeated. 'Caught her with one hand, and put her wig back on with the other.' He paused again. 'That's how I hurt my back. She's a damn sight heavier than she looks.'

He winced again.

'We must have looked a pair, staggering about on the top of that grave, till the others pulled us back.' He looked at me very seriously. 'Wouldn't have done to let her fall in, would it?'

I thought of the last time he had watched her fall in his pig manure, and smiled.

'No, it would not have done,' I agreed.

I examined his spine. It seemed very likely that he had suffered a crush fracture of one of his lower vertebrae. His hips were more or less incapable of movement. There was nothing for it but to admit him to hospital.

He reluctantly agreed. Hurried arrangements were made for someone to feed his pigs and see to his plants, and I admitted him straight from the surgery.

In the hospital, X-rays showed that he had fortunately not suffered a serious crush fracture. Since, with two stiff hips, most of his walking movement was made by rotating his spine, an injured spine rendered him virtually immobile. He agreed with the surgeon that, since he was in hospital, he might just as well have those two new hips fitted while he was at it.

He was in the hospital for almost two months. I went to see him when he came out. From somewhere, he had found a nephew, a younger, cheerful, whistling copy of himself who, delighted to be in charge, had taken over the pigs and the plants. Old George seemed content. For the first time in his life he was having a complete rest, and thoroughly enjoying it.

Very gingerly, with two walking sticks, he took a few steps across the room.

'Doc,' he said, 'have you thought about getting some chicken manure?'

I hadn't. I had abandoned all thoughts of manure. Frank was struggling to get the pruning done, alone. I had discovered that he did not drive a tractor, he was expecting me to do that. I was tending to avoid the farm. It was cold, wet and bleak in December.

'This advert here,' George said, passing over the local farming paper. 'These people will come and spread it for you.'

I read his advert. This large broiler chicken concern, some miles away, who were cleaning out their sheds, for a vast sum of money were prepared to cart the stuff in, and spread it instantly all over the farm.

'There's the phone,' said George. 'Get it now, before someone else does.'

Rashly, I used his telephone. Foolishly, I agreed to take the lot, for that incredibly large sum of money, and agreed that they should come and spread it.

Chicken manure from broiler sheds is dry, very dry, and mixed with the shredded wood shavings of the dry litter, it is like powder. They came to spread it on a very windy day.

In the words of the old song, they flung it here, they flung it there. It was widely distributed. The near gale force wind carried it over a considerable area.

The gale was followed by heavy rain, the effect of which was quite dramatic. The high ammonia content of the manure burnt the leaves off everything it touched.

Later that spring, the strawberries looked magnificent to me. Frank was reticent, not happy, the vibes non-specific, but not good. Old George, despite pressing invitations to come and see the magnificent results of his chicken manure, always somehow declined. I repeatedly reassured him that his new hips would stand it, but he wouldn't come.

Proudly, I took Walter, The Old Boy, to see them.

He carefully put his spade away in the shed, and I took him from the garden, across the road to the strawberry bed.

Solemnly he inspected it. He walked up and down the rows, lifting the vibrant, dark green foliage, and poking about in the middle of the plants. He walked across the field and peered into the centre of some more.

'Well?' I said expectantly.

His verdict is engraved on my brain.

'I don't know about you, Boy, but I don't eat leaves.'

The high nitrogen of the manure, applied too early in the year, had produced a magnificent crop of leaves, at the expense of the fruit buds. That expensive manure had about halved my first strawberry crop.

*   *   *

Chicken muck was out. The next year I tried spent mushroom manure. The thin coating over the ground seemed very expensive for what it was, and the only tangible result that we could see was the finest crop of annual stinging nettles ever grown by anybody, together with the luxuriant widespread growth of a thick-leaved marsh weed that defied every week killer in Frank's book.

I only had to mention manure to see, as well as feel, the hostile vibes emanating from his person.

*   *   *

The coming of his nephew transformed Old George's existence. It had taken him a long time to learn to walk again without sticks. Although the operations on both hips had ben a resounding success, and the surgeon was well pleased with his work, Old George seemed to lack the confidence to walk without his two sticks.

His slightly fractured vertebra had healed completely,

his new hip joints were fully mobile and completely pain-free, and yet, three months after he had returned from hospital, he was still walking with his sticks.

It was merely a question of confidence in walking without them. He had resumed his greenhouse work full time and, seated on his wooden stool, pricked out and potted up his thousands of plants. With one hand securely holding onto his bench, he manipulated heavy bags of potting compost with a practised ease, but he would not let go of the bench to use two hands.

I feared that if we could not break this habit soon, it would become permanent.

His cheerful nephew, permanently whistling, and with a happy smile on his face, took over the pigs completely. He confided to me that his ambition was to 'go big', to have a hundred breeding sows, and big units where a tractor moved the heavy muck and mechanisation moved the food.

'There's money in it, Doc,' he told me. 'But first I've got to earn enough to get started. He kicked the old barrow derisively. 'No money in this way, only hard work, a bad back, and stiff hips.'

George was more than content to watch him wheeling that heavy barrow up and down.

One day, unexpectedly, he asked me directly if I thought he could ever handle that heavy barrow again. I thought of what his nephew had said.

'Yes and no,' I replied. 'You're quite capable of doing it, ought to be doing it, you've been slacking long enough.'

He grinned at me, and began to roll himself another cigarette.

'But?' he said, putting the thin tube of paper between his lips, and groping for his matches.

'You'd be a fool to start,' I said. 'The sheer weight of the thing would wear those hips out so fast, within a year you'd be back to Butazolidine, and bedridden.'

The head of the match scraped slowly over the side of the box. It flared, and he raised it slowly to his face. He had obviously given it a great deal of thought. It struck me quite forcibly, that the reason he was making such slow progress was probably the subconscious knowledge that he did not want to heave that barrow again.

He looked at me over the flame of the match. It was still an inch away from the end of his cigarette, and slowly burning down towards his fingers. With an oath, he threw it down on the floor and rubbed his fingers together.

'Your nephew,' I said, 'wants to go big, throw that barrow away, get mechanised. Why don't you let him?'

He lit another match, and carefully applied it to his cigarette. He took a deep inhalation of smoke.

'I will,' he said, blowing the smoke out.

The decision was made.

'You can start by throwing those sticks away,' I said.

*　　*　　*

The massive sheds were erected. Down a central gangway ran a mechanised sweeper. The muck was moved effortlessly out and away.

I came to an arrangement with George's nephew: I would supply him with all the straw to put under his pigs; in return, he would bring me all the muck, and deposit it in one great big heap at the top of the car park. A contractor would be hired to cart and spread it.

By this time, the whole farm was Pick Your Own, but that is another story.

Muck should be spread in the autumn.

That autumn, the contractor set to work. A conveyor belt of tractors and trailers, with five tons of pig muck on each, rolled up to the fruit farm.

They headed for the designated spot, at the top of the car park, where another massive tractor with a front-end loader waited to pile it high.

Eagerly I looked forward to gloating over that pile of muck, to having my own supply of precious farming life blood.

I had not anticipated that it would be a very rainy autumn. The ground was wet, soft, and muddy.

Leaving them to it, I set off to the surgery.

The first load left deep ruts up the car park. The second load, so as not to make that rut too deep, took a different route up to the heap, and so made a second impression.

When the driver tried to reverse this second load up to the first, the tractor merely dug itself into the ground. He deposited the load where it was, and went back for more.

'It'll all push up together later,' he told Frank cheerfully, as he went off.

The car park was then a little over two acres in size. By lunch-time, one half of it was covered with two hundred tons of steaming muck, in five-ton heaps, and the other half deeply rutted in parallel lines three feet apart, up and down it.

That afternoon, the massive tractor with the front-end loader had dug itself into a large muddy hole, and was there firmly stuck.

A bulldozer was summoned, which carved a track to the first heap, behind which was embedded the front-end loader. This tried to move the first heap to one side, but only succeeded in burying itself without moving the heap an inch.

With many swear words, and churning the mixture of muck and car park soil into an irregular morass, somewhat reminiscent of a First World War battlefield, the two tractors winched each other out.

'We'll come and push it up when the land's dried out a bit,' the driver of the loader called to me, as he went, over the noise of Radio One from his cab.

*   *   *

In the end, most of that muck was sort of incorporated into the structure of the car park in the eventual levelling process. Very little actually found its way onto the strawberries. The only positive result was that we had the lushest grass to park on in the whole of East Anglia. But that came later.

5

The fact that work expands to fill the time available is only too true as far as I am concerned, particularly on Thursday afternoons. According to the appointment book this should have been a very light and easy surgery. Somehow it had turned out not to be. Troubles always come in threes.

Old Granny Hicks had come for a repeat of her usual rheumatic prescriptions. Because we both knew that my appointment system was running early, conversation had ranged much wider than usual, and sitting listening to her talk, I had become increasingly aware that her multiplicity of problems had probably a common origin other than her advanced age.

The more I studied her face, and questioned her about her aches and pains, her slowness of thought, speech and movement, her acute appreciation of the cold, the more it became apparent that not only was she suffering from a deficiency of thyroid, but also that both Mac and I had missed it.

With the light of hindsight it was only too obvious that the condition had crept up on her over the previous year or so. Both of us, seeing her so often, had not noticed the gradual appearance of those significant changes in her skin, her speech and general demeanour.

I arranged for all the usual tests to confirm it, and made sure that she had an appointment to see me the following week.

After she had left the room, I was seated in my chair, feeling half smug that I had noticed it at last, and half contrite that it had taken me so long to do so, when the next patient walked in.

Thyroid disease was on my mind.

'Sit down, Mrs Bliss,' I said, looking at the same time at her son, whom she had brought with her. I hadn't seen him for a year or so, and there was definitely something amiss. He was a gangling youth of twelve, but somehow looked bigger than he should. Without actually moving, he appeared all on the twitch.

'Good morning, Robert,' I said to him.

He seemed to stare back at me unblinking. I stood up: he looked up at me. I sat down: his eyes followed me downwards, and then slowly the eyelids followed his eyes. It was the definite lid lag of thyrotoxicosis.

It was unbelievable to have two successive cases of thyroid disease in one surgery.

While his mother was talking I looked for, and saw, the protuberant eyes, the typical fine tremor of the hands, the loss of weight, the apparent inability to concentrate. Yes, he was quite literally all on the twitch.

With some impatience I waited for his mother to finish telling me all about it. Subconsciously, I had heard her while my mind was occupied with looking at Robert. She had brought him, in essence, because his performance at school had suddenly gone off. Whereas he used to be a bright boy, his most recent reports had been bad. His teacher had raised the subject of unhappiness at home as a possible cause. Loudly and indignantly protesting at the slur cast on her home and her marriage, Mrs Bliss had come to seek retribution, help and advice.

Eventually she finished. 'Pop on the couch,' I told Robert, and to his astonished mother I pointed out the signs of excessive thyroid hormone.

'How long has he been like this?' I asked her.

'About a year,' she replied.

I was acutely conscious that during the same year I had completely missed old Granny Hicks's deterioration.

'I should have brought him a long time ago, then?' she said.

'Yes,' I agreed, wondering to myself whether, if she had, I would have noticed it. The early changes of thyroid gland disease are so easy to miss, while it literally stares you in the face when well established.

We talked for a while, and I explained to them both what it was all about, and how Robert would be restored to complete normality. I explained how the diagnosis must be confirmed with some blood tests, and arranged for these to be done. She listened avidly as I told her that the first treatment was a course of pills, which would probably be all that was required. I also mentioned that in a few cases, the condition recurred after the course of treament, and that in these cases an operation, to remove the part of his thyroid gland that was over-producing, might be needed in the future.

'So it's got nothing to do with unhappiness at home?' she said, when I had finished.

'Nothing,' I agreed.

'Just wait till I get hold of that schoolteacher,' she muttered, with a gleam of righteous indignation in her eye. 'I'm going to pin him up against a wall, in public, at playtime, and I'm going to tell him the facts of life.'

Grabbing hold of Robert's hand and marching him towards the door, she stopped, and turning forcefully, announced at me, but to the world in general, 'He accused me of having an unhappy home, never noticing all that while that my son was ill, and needed an operation.'

She marched out. Like so many of us, she had turned the guilty feelings of not having noticed the severity of her son's condition, into aggression towards someone else who hadn't noticed either, but who now, in her opinion, bore the total responsibility for the omission. Her conscience was clear: it was all his fault. She was in reality over-compensating to cover the truth that her home was not one of the happiest.

'Come back next week for the results of the tests,' I called after her retreating form.

I was now almost expecting the hat trick, a third case of thyroid disease.

Intently I scanned the features of the next patient as he walked in. The record card in my hand was blank. He was a new patient, and apart from the fact that his name was Sylvester Jones, there was no other information. My appointment system was now an hour out, and he was not pleased.

There was that look of 'I am a busy, important man, and you have kept me waiting' on his face, but no sign of thyroid disorder, only displeasure superimposed on the plumpness of good living.

Feeling almost disappointed, I invited him to come in and sit down.

I waited for him to speak. Almost embarrassed and unsure of himself, half-cocksure and self-important, he began.

'I am the new chief clerk to Thorpe and Goodman,' he said.

I had heard, from another patient, that this firm of solicitors in town had indeed recently appointed a new chief clerk. The new man had been described to me as 'a bumptious little toad from London'. My informant had been his predecessor, who had been compulsorily retired on his seventieth birthday, against his better feelings. He had been overheard to dismiss his successor contemptuously as 'jumped up', while clearing his desk of a lifetime's memories, before he walked out, into an empty and bitter retirement.

'I suffer from hypertension,' announced the new chief clerk, as he sat down. 'I would like you to check my blood pressure.

'Surely,' I said, as I looked at him. Aged about thirty, more than somewhat overweight, he returned my look through a pair of thick, horn-rimmed glasses. He was tallish, and beginning to go bald on top. I gained the impression of a fussy, somewhat pedantic man, a man who chased detail till it was all accounted for.

I measured his pressure and listened to his heart. Although the pressure was raised a little, his heart and the rest of him were very normal. The only significant thing to find medically was that, with his shirt off, he was much fatter than he appeared with it on.

'Are you taking any medicines?' I asked him, not expecting him to say that he was.

To my surprise, he produced three different sorts of anti-hypertensive pills, and placing them carefully on the table, turned the labels towards me so that I could read them.

One was a mild tranquilliser, one a sleeping pill, and the third a mild diuretic. Only the last could be deemed to be a genuine blood pressure pill.

'My own doctor –' he paused for emphasis – 'in Harley Street –' pausing again slightly, making sure that I had understood the implications of the address – 'said that I would need to take these for life.'

'Oh, yes,' I said. 'Were you under a lot of stress at the time?'

'Yes,' he said, 'quite a bit.'

He looked surprised that I had asked the question. I did not tell him that my informant had somewhat maliciously stated the reason for his seeking a change of employment, so far from his previous job.

He looked up at me across the desk. 'I worked for a very busy firm of solicitors in London,' he admitted. 'Too busy really, too many partners. I was promoted too soon, things got a bit out of hand.'

The half-cocksure had given way to the half-embarrassed.

'I think here, in a smaller firm, for a few years, then I shall be ready for the big time again.'

Roughly the same information had been supplied across this same desk in a much more derogatory fashion.

I nodded my head sympathetically.

He continued, 'My wife . . . our marriage . . . it was a sticky patch, the other man, you know.'

My informant had stated categorically that there had been an embarrassing liaison with one of the junior partners.

I nodded again, in sympathy.

'What about your weight?' I asked, changing the subject.

He shrugged his shoulders.

'You will probably find,' I told him, 'that once you and your wife settle in here, the pace of life in East Anglia is such that your pressure will come down quite markedly. Cut out the stress, lose three stone in weight, and you will probably not need those Harley Street pills.'

He smiled in a somewhat superior fashion. 'We'll see,' he said.

I arranged for the usual basic blood tests, X-rays and cardiograph to be done, and asked him to make a further appointment next week. The expression on his face showed that he had not expected such sophisticated facilities to be available so far out in the provinces.

The remainder of that Thursday afternoon surgery was as quick and uneventful as I had been expecting it all to be, and I was soon through it.

The following Thursday, I noted with some surprise that the first three patients were a repeat of the previous week.

Grandma Hicks was indeed very short of thyroid. I started her on the replacement therapy, and told her to make an appointment for four weeks hence. Somehow it took much longer than planned. She had hardly understood a word, or had forgotten all the explaining done last week.

'You must start off with a tiny dose,' I told her, 'and work up gradually to the full amount. If you take the full dose all at once, it will make you feel awful.' I had thought she had understood.

60

Robert Bliss's blood test showed that he had far too much. His thyroid was much too active. I started him on the antithyroid drug – again, a small dose and work up – explaining to his mother that he would need regular blood tests to check on his response to the therapy.

His mother was not really listening. She was far too busy telling me all about her encounter with the schoolmaster, who had accused her of having an unsatisfactory marriage. The longer she went on, the more sympathy I felt for the schoolmaster, and the more I realised that he did indeed have a very good insight into Robert's home life.

I showed her the door with relief. 'See you in four weeks,' I said.

Sylvester Jones came in. All his blood tests were completely normal, as was his X-ray. The cardiograph showed not the slightest evidence of any of the changes due to high blood pressure.

Once again I had a long and earnest discussion about the best way to treat his condition. Once more I explained that if he lost some weight and took more exercise, I was certain he could be weaned off the pills.

'You mean, you approve of the alternative medicine?' he said, at the end of it.

'No,' I replied. 'This is common sense.'

'Will jogging be a satisfactory form of exercise?' he asked, getting all his details straight.

'Very satisfactory,' I said.

I sat for a moment or two in my chair. Once more my Thursday afternoon surgery was running an hour late.

I began to dread Thursdays. There they all were, the following week, all booked in as extra emergencies at the beginning of the session. Each one had persuaded the receptionist that they would only take a minute.

Granny Hicks was accompanied by her equally aged husband. On the basis that he had once treated vitamin deficiency in his pigs with a massive loading dose, followed by regular maintenance, he had pronounced that the same principles applied to thyroids. They were, after all, only vitamins.

He had administered most of the bottle in one glorious swallow, and please could they now have some more.

Granny was just starting to get the shakes, the anxiety, and the phobias. Her pulse was running at one hundred and twenty. There was a high probability that she would go into heart failure, and an even higher probability that she would develop the myxoedema madness of too sudden a correction. There was nothing I could do, except pray, and not give her any more till next week.

Grandpa Hicks was not convinced by my explanation, or my anger, and went off muttering.

An unwilling Robert was dragged in by his irate mother. She was already fed up with having to give him all those pills. Arguments were raging at home about taking time off for the weekly blood test, which in their opinion wasn't necessary anyway. Couldn't he have the operation now, and be done with it? Quite in passing, she was going to sue that schoolmaster. He had been very rude.

Once again I tried to explain, but I was talking to a closed pair of ears, until, still protesting, she was ushered to the door. Robert was very embarrassed. He was quite happy to take pills. An operation defnitely did not appeal.

Sylvester Jones rose from his chair in the waiting room, and limped painfully through the consulting room door.

Whilst on his first jog, he had strained his knee. He merely wished to know the best method of bandaging it up. He had apparently tried to run ten miles on his first outing. Most of the outward leg had been done at walking pace, the return journey at a painful hobble. Incredibly, he was still enthusiastic. We had a long talk on the principles of athletic fitness, and how it made sense to start off gently, warm up, and slowly increase the speed and the distance.

Exactly one week later, Thursday afternoon, they were all back again.

Granny Hicks was quite demented, but only racing at the hundred. The old man accused me of poisoning her. He was not going to let her take any of those damn thyroid pills ever again.

The thiouracil tablets I had given young Robert hadn't made the slightest difference so far: he needed a higher dose. A truce had been declared at school, but the narration of the terms took longer than the negotiations themselves.

My appointment system was already an hour late when Sylvester Jones made his entrance. His knee was improving but 'could I just spare a moment to check his training programme?'

I did. It took half an hour.

When Thursday came round again, so did the terrible trio.

Granny Hicks had moments of lucidity, and a pulse rate of ninety. She was somewhat short of breath, with swollen ankles. Her poor old heart needed a bit of help.

I argued, wheedled, cajoled and dictated, going through the thyroid dose all over again. Grandpa eventually took the prescription reluctantly. Despite my insistence, grave doubts remained as to whether he would actually give his wife the pills. He, on his part, had lost his faith in doctors.

Robert had had his weekly blood test. Unfortunately, the blood had not been taken cleanly, and he had developed a huge, ugly, lumpy bruise in his elbow. It was uncomfortable and unsightly, but needed no active treatment. It would clear up on its own over the next week.

I explained to him how to prevent such a thing happening again, by holding his arm up above his head, after the blood had been taken. He understood how this would take the pressure off the vein wall, but his mother was not listening. She would not permit such assaults on her offspring ever again. Why couldn't he have the operation and be done with it?

Sylvester Jones was progressing through his training

63

manual. He had found, in the second-hand bookshop, what appeared to be the perfect book on sensible dieting. Could I just check its validity?

I did. It took half an hour.

The next week, I found out why they all came on Thursday afternoons: it was early closing day.

For the Hickses, it meant that the buses were not crowded. Her heart failure was controlled, and it was almost time to reintroduce a small maintenance dose of thyroid. She had now regained enough of her mental faculties to argue as well, but not enough to be entirely logical. It was very difficult.

Mrs Bliss did not work on Thursdays. Robert had responded too well to the pills, and I had to reduce the dose right back. Mrs Bliss was still quite vocal, and her opinions forcefully expressed.

Sylvester Jones was coming on quite nicely. Since he went into the office on a Saturday morning, to deal with the mail, he had Thursday afternoons off instead. His weight was dropping, his sense of well-being improved, and his blood pressure entirely normal. We had another long chat about the advisability of coming off his medication too soon. He agreed tentatively to drop the odd pill, and see how it went. His knee still twinged.

Slowly, as the weeks and months went by, all situations came under control. It seemed that on most Thursdays at least, one of the trio was there. Eventually, Grandma Hicks and I were able to laugh at the catastrophic effects of her husband's limited therapeutic knowledge, though he maintained a dignified and aloof silence. Her rheumatic pains had dramatically gone, she felt alive, and declared she had lost twenty years. Physically, she was very well.

Young Robert, too, responded satisfactorily. His twitching stopped, he put on weight, and his work at school improved by leaps and bounds.

Their attendance in the surgery dropped to routine check visits, but still always on a Thursday afternoon.

Sylvester Jones was not so fortunate. Although his weight and blood pressure were very satisfactory, he had great difficulty in coming off the tranquillisers. We both realised that he had become addicted to them, but with help and perseverance he overcame it. He became addicted to jogging instead, and developed into a real fitness fanatic.

The pains in his knee persisted, and I began to suspect that he could have damaged the cartilage within it, particularly when the knee stuck in the half bent position, and he had to perform wriggling contortions to get it straight again.

He sent for me at home one evening. His knee had completely locked on him, and he was utterly unable to straighten it. It was very painful. The torn cartilage had moved and got stuck in the joint, and no amount of wiggling could free it. There was nothing for it but to admit him directly to hospital, for an operation to remove the torn cartilage.

He was not a good patient, and the operation did not go well. He had a lot of bleeding into the joint cavity afterwards, so convalescence was slow and prolonged.

Once he came home, his knee was still far too painful for jogging, and he began to fret at his lack of fitness.

'Can you ride a bicycle? I suggested. 'Non-weightbearing exercise could be very helpful.'

His eyes lit up, and in no time at all he had acquired an old machine and went cycling with the same determination that he had put into jogging. During the period of his convalescence, he cycled twenty or thirty miles a day.

He sat in the surgery, again by habit on a Thursday afternoon, and we discussed his fitness to return to work.

'Do you mind if I stay off a big longer?' he asked diffidently. 'I know that my knee is virtually right, but I'm standing on it most of the time at work, and it still aches if I spend more than a few minutes with my weight on it.'

'Not at all,' I replied. His knee was still a bit inflamed,

with a residual effusion. It certainly did need more time to heal. Had he said that he could cope with his work, I would have signed him off as fit to do so, since whatever he did now, his knee would ultimately heal.

'It's funny,' he said. 'I can't stand, but I can cycle miles, with no pain at all.' He looked earnestly across the desk at me. 'For the first time in my life, I am wandering up all these country lanes, and actually seeing what is there. All those different species of birds. In a car, all you see is the road and the car in front, but on a bicycle, I am in a new world.'

He grinned at me. 'To be honest, I'm enjoying not working.' He paused, and his face became serious. 'All my life,' he said, 'has been spent in the town, first at school, and then in a solicitor's office. Work was always the important thing, it always came first. This is all new to me, I'm just beginning to realise what I've been missing all this time.'

I gave him a further certificate for another two weeks.

'I'm going to try and buy a cottage in the country,' he said as he left.

Two weeks later, again on a Thursday afternoon, he came into the surgery for his final sign-off. Somehow, once more, I was running over an hour late. Mistakenly, I presumed that this would be a quick consultation.

'I've found my cottage,' he announced, as he walked in.

'Oh yes?' I said, pointing to the couch. He climbed on it, and I examined his knee. The fluid had gone, and he had recovered full movement.

'No pain now?' I asked.

'None at all,' he said.

I scribbled the relevant words on a certificate, that he was now fully fit to resume work, and placed it within his reach on the desk.

He did not pick it up, but sat down in the chair beside the desk instead.

'It's at the far end of your village,' he said, 'you must know it. The cottage next to Old Jack's, the gamekeeper.

Old Jack was a dour old man, a Scot like Mac. I hardly knew him. He had retired from gamekeeping years ago, and whatever medication he needed, Mac provided. He was extremely old, but famed for his taxidermy. He had been stuffing birds all his life.

'I was out cycling, and found this dead bird in the road. It had been hit by a car, and someone suggested that I take it to Old Jack.'

He paused in his narrative. Hopefully I pushed the certificate in his direction. His knee was obviously better. There was every indication that it was going to be another long, tiring Thursday afternoon. He ignored my gesture.

'Old Jack got quite excited,' he said. 'The bird was a hawk, one called a hobby. He'd not seen one since he left Scotland. They're very rare, apparently. He's going to show me how to stuff it.'

'That's when you saw the cottage was for sale?' I said.

'Yes,' he said. 'It's not really as big as we would like, but we've agreed to buy it.'

Gently I prodded the certificate towards him. 'Your knee's fully recovered, I presume?' I said.

'Oh yes, thanks. Old Jack told me you kept ducks. He asked me to say that if any die, could he have them to stuff?'

'Certainly,' I said, standing up and handing him the certificate. 'I'll definitely let you know if any ducks die.'

He marched briskly and happily off. Even with the last of the trio no longer a regular attender, Thursday afternoons were still running very late.

I rang the bell for the next patient.

6

As I looked across the kitchen table at the young man, trying to size him up, it was the whites of his eyes that were remarkable. They were clear and shining, brilliant ultra-white.

When he smiled, his eyelids opened that little bit extra so that the whiteness shone out, as if he had been lit up. His teeth had the white evenness of youth, too, so that, surrounded by a full red mouth and covered by a dark dago moustache, the flash of them in the smile was an irresistible sexual signal.

His dress was deliberately, and studiedly, casual. An open-neck check shirt and wide leather belt with ornamental buckle superbly complemented his long, straight limbs in the skin-tight blue jeans.

He looked as if he was only too aware of the effect he thought he had on susceptible members of the opposite sex, but I imagined that mature women would find him brash and empty. I felt that, after the first strong impressions, there would not be a lot behind the façade. He struck me as a loner, a superficial young man with few friends.

I was not at that moment interested in that side of his character, however. All I wanted to know was whether he could drive a tractor. He had applied to the fruit farm for a job.

It was coming up spring, and we were desperate for a tractor driver. We had been only too aware that one would be needed ever since we had taken possession of the farm the previous October.

It had been high summer when the purchase of the farm had been agreed, but in the traditional manner, money did not actually change hands till Michaelmas, which gave Sir Percival time to harvest and sell the last of the vegetables and apples before we took over the land and the trees.

During that first long, wet winter, the fact that Frank could not drive a tractor had not mattered. All the pruning that had kept him so busy had been hand work, but now that the spring had come, the prunings needed sweeping up, and most of the farm needed hoeing, spraying or fertilising. There was an incredible programme of preventative spraying and weedkiller application to be done.

Frank was now insistent that he was two weeks behind already.

'Couldn't you try to learn to drive the tractor?' I begged him. 'Look, I can do it. I'll show you how.'

But he was adamant. 'Doctor,' he said with great dignity, 'I am now sixty-six. At your request I have stayed on to help you with this first year. I have never driven a tractor in my life, and feel that I'm too old to start now.'

I realised that he could not be pressed any further. I knew that if I pushed him, he would quietly hand me in his notice and draw his well-deserved old age pension. I should then have nobody who knew the slightest thing about fruit growing, and I had so much to learn.

Throughout that winter he had done all the pruning alone. It had been a prodigous task. I had not appreciated what quite incredible amounts of vegetation had to be removed from apple trees and black currant bushes. Removing all last year's thorny growth from blackberries, raspberries, and so on, seemed to take away more than was left. The rows between the plants were waist-high with it.

At times, I had helped him to move some of it out of the way, so that he could get on with the essential winter spraying. I drove one of the tractors, but my efforts were amateur, and mainly not available when he needed them. He could direct and guide superbly: he knew the exact speeds and pressures for the machines to put the chemicals

69

on the land, but refused resolutely to steer any form of mechanical contrivance down the rows. It was very frustrating, and explained why the two of us were now sitting in the kitchen, interviewing potential tractor drivers on a Sunday morning, when we both had better things to do.

At least, we had hoped to be interviewing potential tractor drivers. The young man with the flashing eyes was the only applicant. He gave me a beaming smile.

I asked him his name.

'Rupert,' he replied. 'Rupert Bigelow.'

He had a strong Midlands accent, not local at all. It clashed with Frank's soft Suffolk. I could feel that Frank was not enthusiastic. He would never actually show disapproval, he merely emitted soft, negative Suffolk vibes.

'How long have you been driving tractors?' he asked after we had been chatting for a while.

'Most of my life, really,' the young man said casually. 'I grew up in a small village, where it's natural to drive tractors.'

He smiled, and the teeth and eyes flashed white. 'That is, until we moved here, of course,' he said. 'I've been doing a bit of this and a bit of that since then.'

He did not say what, and I didn't ask him.

'Have you ever done any spraying?' asked Frank.

'No,' Rupert admitted honestly, 'but I'm willing to learn.'

I looked at Frank and caught his eye. His expression was exactly neutral.

'What do you think?' I said, pushing him.

He remained exactly neutral – no help at all. I had to make the decision myself.

Rupert smiled at me, those extra-white conjunctivae of his somehow disarming.

'Do you think you can do the job?' I asked.

The smile flashed again.

'Frank?' I said, waiting a long time for his opinion. Benignly, Frank maintained his soft Suffolk neutrality. I could feel the vibes coming through. He did not think much of Rupert, but it was him or nothing.

Frank did not speak, while Rupert flashed the smile again at both of us, utterly unaware of Frank's vibes.

'Do you want the job?' I said.

'Yes, please,' he said.

So, against all our better judgement, I gave him the job and we now had a tractor driver. A very inexperienced tractor driver, but one who was willing to learn. He would be taught by an old man who knew the end results he wanted, and how to achieve them, but who utterly and resolutely refused to drive the tractor himself.

Initially, all went well. Rupert had a chance to refresh his basic skills, and get his hand back in, by pushing out all the prunings. This was done by a buckrake on the back of the tractor, reversing the tractor up the rows, so that the horizontal metal prongs of the buckrake gathered the prunings up into great heaps and carted them off to be burned.

Several times he wrapped the buckrake round a few of the trees. Not often enough to do really serious damage, but enough for Frank to indicate, in his quiet way, extreme displeasure. Rupert's empty, flashing, sexual smile did not help.

It became painfully obvious, as the weeks passed, that they did not get on, they tolerated each other as necesasary evils. They had very little to say to each other, apart from the essentials of job communication. Frank had very little respect for Rupert, but as neither of them complained to me, and they seemed to be getting through all the busy routine of farm work, I made no comment to either of them.

Spring was the season of strawberry spraying. Frank was adamant that, without his tight schedule of multiple preventative chemical spraying, there would be no strawberry crop. His shopping list of chemicals was almost as long as my pharmacopoeia. Fruiting plants seemed to have more diseases than the human race, and infinitely more remedies for their cure and prevention. My mind just could not take in the incredible complexity of it. In some ways it was worse than going back to medical school again.

As the spring arrived, I came to have an immense sympathy for those strawberries. They sat there, in rows, mute, silent, and uncomplaining.

Into their oxygen-starved, waterlogged roots, the red-core and mycelium fungi grew unchecked. Nematode worms chewed quite happily into them, and the plants never said a word.

Above ground the aphids, whitefly, red spiders and caterpillars sucked their juices and ate their leaves, while within them various virus reversions undermined their capacity to produce fruit, and turned their leaves yellow. Innumerable deficiency diseases wreaked their havoc.

Not only that, but as soon as a fruit bud appeared from the depths of the plant, a queue of different insects, moulds, birds and assorted other pests appeared, to attack it.

According to the chemical companies, it was a miracle if Mother Nature produced a single edible strawberry unaided. And all this time, those plants never said a word, never complained once, never sent for me in the middle of the night; just lay back and took it.

They never once complained of side effects, never once became allergic to all that assorted medication sprayed over, into and under them. They didn't even squeal when Rupert drove his huge tractor wheels down the rows, instead of between them. The fruit just squashed and went mouldy, silently, while Frank and I swore.

I spent hours communing with them, recovering from the vociferous demands of the human race. Their uncomplaining silence was soothing, as I inspected and sympathised with their innumerable wounds and sores.

'It's time to put the straw out,' Frank said one Friday

lunchtime. A sort of ritual had developed on Friday lunchtime. Frank and Rupert came over to the house to be paid every Friday. After the pay packets had been handed over and last week's overtime carefully written down, it was time to discuss the programme for next week. I learned whether things were behind or ahead of schedule, what wanted doing urgently, and what could wait till next week.

All the spraying had to be done by mid-May. After that it was time to get the straw-laying done.

The straw was already in the barn, delivered straight off the baler last harvest, fresh from the field. It had arrived before I took over; the bill for it arrived later, after I had. A mere detail like change of ownership didn't upset the time-honoured rituals and arrangements. Frank assured me that it had indeed been ordered, and checked – so I paid.

It was now time to put it out. I had thought that the easiest way to get the straw under the plants was to chop it up into short lengths with a forage harvester, load it, like silage, into the muck cart, and then spread it over the field.

I explained my ideas to Frank. 'If we put it on in the autumn, straight off the harvest field, it will act as a mulch and kill all those weeds, and the strawberries will grow through it, saving all that work.'

He was horrified. Dire references were made to botrytis and spring frosts killing all the blossom. That was definitely not on. The straw should be placed under the blossom, after it had received all its preventative anti-mould sprays, and after all danger of late spring frosts had passed.

'Shall I get the women in?' he asked. There was only the slightest pause before he said, 'I've told most of them to come on Monday.' The vibes of his body language said very plainly that this was not a matter for discussion.

So it was agreed. I didn't know how many he would need, or how much to pay them; all I knew was that, from time immemorial, his wife Daisy had been in charge. She would hire and fire, set the rate of pay, and I would hand over the necessary money every teatime.

I sneaked a few moments off after Monday morning surgery, and between visits walked over to the strawberry field. Old Walter came with me, carrying his spade.

Dotted here and there among the strawberries were isolated clumps of largish weeds – mainly docks, thistles, and stinging nettles. These had not responded to the routine weedkillers, so Frank had asked Old Walter to come over and dig them out. I had not been consulted, but had to agree that the field would look much neater and tidier without them.

It was a lovely May morning, with hardly a cloud in the sky. The sun warmed us as we ambled over the car park and down to the strawberry field.

Frank and Rupert were ferrying the straw bales out of the barn on the buckrake on the back of the tractor. They then placed them carefully down the rows, ready for the women to cut the strings, and shake handfuls of straw under the emerging fruit trusses.

There must have been thirty women in the field, of all ages, shapes and sizes. A few I knew, and exchanged greetings with them. Most were complete strangers, who either ignored me or acknowledged my presence with a shy, or a casual nod. Most had come strawing for years. They worked for Daisy and Frank, not me. I was superfluous.

All, bar one, wore a sort of uniform – a baggy old pair of trousers, an equally scruffy long-sleeved shirt, and an old headscarf to keep off the sun, and keep the straw out of their hair. They knelt on the earth, shaking out the straw, and shuffling forward over their work to the next clump of straw laid ready for them by Rupert and Frank.

The one not wearing the uniform was an attractive young lady, bareheaded and, in contrast to the others, virtually nude. She had on a very short pair of shorts, a bare midriff, and a very loose, precariously tied headscarf around her well-developed bosom.

Unlike the others, she worked standing up, her short little shorts riding high up her buttocks, and her headscarf hanging down, barely covering her indecency.

Old Walter was shocked and speechless. Rupert was definitely switched on. His neon light of a smile flashed repeatedly in her direction, and her come-hither glances back were quite definitely putting his mind off his work. Frank was emitting quite audible negative vibes.

'Where'd you get that one from?' I asked him in a whisper.

'Lives in the village,' he hissed back. 'She'd got clothes on when she asked Daisy for a job.'

As far as I could see, she was working as well as everybody else and, apart from the consternation she was causing among the male side of the workforce, was having no detrimental effect on the other women. They seemed particularly unbothered as they got on with their work.

I left the two old men to their muttering, and returned to my Monday hospital round.

'You see, come tomorrow, she'll be decent,' I heard Frank say. 'That's scratchy old stuff, straw.'

'True,' Old Walter agreed. 'Come morning, she'll be so sore, she'll be covering it up.'

On Tuesday, it was such a glorious day, I envied them all working out in the fields while I had to spend most of the day indoors. I rushed through my morning surgery and day's visits, in order to have a little time in the field myself.

A very considerable area had been covered with straw. Frank was well content. Rupert was working really hard, not only at carting straw, but also simultaneously impressing the womenfolk with his muscles and his dexterity.

The naked flesh had not been covered up. Her legs and arms were quite red with the irritation from the straw, and all the other bare skin was showing signs of too much exposure to the sun. A thin film of dust clung to her perspiring body, smeared into messy streaks, where she had scratched and rubbed the irritation.

Old Walter, methodically digging out his thistles, actually paused and leaned on his spade to talk to me, as I walked up to him.

'Hot, isn't it?' I said conversationally.

He agreed. His acknowledgement of the heat had been to take his jacket off. His waistcoat was still firmly buttoned over his overalls and his thick cotton shirt.

He nodded in the direction of the bare, exposed legs. She was still standing, bending right over to lay her straw, so that the whole of her long legs, right up to her plump little bottom, was exposed to his gaze. The headscarf round her chest hung tantalisingly down, moving gently to and fro as she pushed in the handfuls of straw.

'It's indecent,' he snorted. 'Her and that Rupert. They ought to be locked up.'

I smiled. It was not an unattractive sight.

'She'll be sore tonight,' he said with some satisfaction. 'Look at her.'

I looked. At that moment Rupert came up with more straw. White teeth and whites of eyes in a very dirty face flashed at her. Slowly she stood up, and smiled back. I could feel the electricity between them.

After a moment, Rupert moved away.

'It's disgusting,' Old Walter muttered. 'And her a married woman.'

He resumed his job of digging out thistles, his slow rhythm a little faster, the venom vented on the thistle roots as he jerked them from the earth.

I walked back, chatting to some of the other women as I passed. The old hands were well protected from the sun, the dust and the straw scratches. Their uniform was sensible protective clothing. Like the old men said, I thought, she'll learn.

I was very surprised to see her towards the end of Wednesday morning surgery. She had been squeezed in as an emergency.

'Hallo,' I said to her in recognition, not realising until this moment that she was a patient, as well as a temporary straw-laying employee. 'I wasn't expecting to see you this morning. Come in, sit down.'

Her record card was on the desk in front of me. I picked it up and read her details as she seated herself gingerly in the chair.

'Thank you,' she said.

Her name was Moira Jones, address 'Gamekeepers' Cottages'.

'Ah,' I said, 'I know your husband, Sylvester Jones. The solicitors' managing clerk, the trainee taxidermist. I've got you placed now.'

'Yes,' she said, smiling in recognition.

'How's his taxidermy going?' I asked, as I began to open the folder of notes, for her medical history.

'Very smelly, and not very well,' she said, laughingly. 'He can't get enough corpses to practise on. He asked me to remind you, that if any of your ducks die, can he have the bodies?'

'Certainly,' I said, glancing at her notes at the same time. There were not a lot of entries. She had led a healthy life.

'Tell me about it, what's the problem today?'

'Your straw,' she said. 'Nobody told me it was dirty, itchy stuff. I'm covered in a rash.'

'Slip your things off, hop on the couch, and let me look,' I said.

She was wearing a longish dress, with a high neck, and long sleeves. Her face and hands, although glowing red with the newly acquired suntan, did not look untoward. She pulled the dress up over her head, walked the few steps to the couch and lay down.

Underneath the dress she was totally naked. Her whole body was bright red, itchy and weeping, with a combination of sunburn, dust allergy and prickly heat.

'Didn't they warn you, on the farm, to keep your skin covered up?' I asked.

77

'Yes,' she said, 'but I thought it was because I was sunbathing. Your two old men got ever so cross.'

She smiled.

'Perhaps I was a bit naughty teasing them. They were so oldfashioned and disapproving.'

I gave her a prescription for some cortisone and antibiotic cream.

'That should clear it up pretty quickly,' I told her, 'but for goodness' sake, don't expose yourself to the sun like that again.'

'Can I go back to work?' she asked. 'I'm nearly out of my mind with boredom, just staring at the walls of that little cottage all day.'

'Why not?' I answered. 'As long as you wear a dress like the one you've got on now, and be like the other women who've done it all before. Get yourself a pair of loose, baggy trousers as well.'

By Friday lunchtime the strawing was almost finished. Frank expressed himself well satisfied with the progress.

'I don't know what you said to that girl,' he remarked, as he and Rupert walked away after our weekly discussion and pay time. 'She was much better dressed when she came back after seeing you in the surgery.'

'Good,' I said, noncommitally. 'How did she work?'

'She's a good little worker,' he admitted, half grudgingly. 'When the strawing's finished, I want to keep a few on, to tie up the raspberry canes, and trim out the summer shoots on the apple trees.'

I don't know how Moira persuaded him, but somehow, she was among the few that he kept on. Perhaps it was because she now wore a long dress, with floppy pyjama-type trousers, or perhaps it was because she was a good little worker, or perhaps it was because the other women all moved on to the Birdseye factory for the pea season which was now opening. In any event, the workforce now consisted of several part-time women, who came and went at Frank's direction.

He informed me how much each one had earned at every Friday lunchtime.

At first she wore her uniform all the time, but I soon began to notice that on warm days she was back to the very short shorts and halter handkerchief. Nobody grumbled, and she did not consult me about the rash, so I left matters well alone.

Only Old Walter, calmly viewing Rupert flashing his smile at her, muttered about troubles ahead.

The fruit grew and swelled in the summer sun and rain. I discussed with Frank arrangements for collecting the money from those who picked their own. It seemed to me logical that he and Rupert should do it.

He positively oozed negative vibes. 'No, Doctor,' he said very quietly. 'I don't think you should let young Rupert handle money. Wouldn't do at all.' It was the first and only criticism he had ever actually made. It was not advice to disregard.

It was time to scour the practice for the selling gang, a few to-be-trusted old age pensioners, looking for amusement and part-time employment.

7

Once more that crow had beaten me. In helpless rage I looked at the ravished duck's nest, and swore. A litter of broken shells and smears of bloodstained yolk were all that was left of another clutch of precious teal eggs. We had several different species of exotic teal. They liked our lake, had settled well to breed, but to date, had hidden their nests so well that we only found them after the crow had destroyed the nest. It was beyond being annoying, it was becoming catastrophic.

The courtship of our most precious birds, the Baikal teal, had been very private and subdued, and mostly done under a bush. Otherwise they were to be seen perched for long hours on an old, half-submerged log, just looking furtive.

As the spring had gathered pace and the apples and strawberries come into flower, so we had dared to hope that they might breed. The Baikal were surely paired, and she was definitely getting heavy with eggs. They spent more and more time hidden from view under the bramble bushes overhanging the lake. After a while, he seemed to sit for most of the day alone on his log, looking mutely glorious, while she had disappeared. She was definitely nesting somewhere, in the rushes over the water, buried deep in a tussock of grass, or even in a hole in a tree.

Desperately we searched, and so did the crow. Morning and evening he sailed lugubriously round the banks of the lake, always seeming to know just when I could not be there with the gun in my hand. Most of the unprotected nests he found first, only leaving the ducks and me the scattered remains of the egg shells in the desecrated nest.

When he had had a really good feed, there was a definite note of satisfaction in the coarse 'caw, caw', as heavily his slow-seeming wings took him up and over the marsh, his crop distended with the half-formed baby ducks so recently still inside their eggs. Old Walter hated it, too. I only hoped that this latest nest he had destroyed was not that of the Baikal. They were far too valuable just to be a snack for an evil-looking crow.

Old Walter really hated them. 'Black b——s are unlucky,' he said, as yet again he saw it heaving itself away. 'Don't like 'um. Never have.'

He did not elaborate. He did not need to. Not only were the crow's raids financially unlucky for us, it made me feel physically sick to see that evil black shape flap away, knowing that it was leaving such a trail of vandalism behind it. It seemed there was no way I could stop it eating our precious duck eggs, and the more it found to eat, the more it returned, and the more diligently it searched for those so far hidden. Every time it was seen around the lake I would rush out with the gun, but always it saw me coming, and although I had fired at it in desperation several times, all I had succeeded in doing was make it even more wary. It did not take it long to learn my working timetable, and it seemed to wait, hidden somewhere just out of sight, till it saw my car go down the drive. With the coast thus clear, it then spent a very profitable morning hunting for my hidden nests. Ruth cried tears over the wanton destruction it caused, and recruited Old Walter to help keep a wary eye open for it, but it spite of their vigilance, it always seemed to creep in unnoticed, and would caw a hoot of derision and victory as it flapped heavily away.

Since there seemed no way of catching or killing it, we tried to scheme up methods of deterrence, to stop it eating eggs. Each one was more bizarre than the last, and none of them worked. I discussed the problem with Old Walter one lunchtime. He shook his head negatively over our latest scheme to poison and deter the crow.

'Had a cockerel once,' he told me as he leaned on his spade in the front border, drinking the tea I had just brought him. 'He was a sod. Ate the eggs as fast as the hens laid um.' He passed me back the mug. 'Cured him in the end, I did.'

One of the things that endeared me to Old Walter was his ability to talk and work. Without altering the flow of his tale, he pushed his spade into the ground, leaned heavily on it with his foot, and then eased the sod of earth forwards. There was a slow, dignified rhythm to it, as he progressed round the garden. I could dig much faster than he did, but needed to pause much more frequently to rest and recuperate, so that at the end of a day his total effort, despite his age, more than matched mine. Most people, including me, stop digging when they talk. Not Old Walter: slowly he continued turning the earth over.

'The wife filled an egg with mustard once,' he said. 'That old cock only ever had one beakful.'

'Did it stop him eating eggs?' I asked. We had indeed tried that remedy for the crow, and had left dozens of doctored eggs out for him, filled with all sorts of nasty stuff. The crow ignored them all.

'Stopped him eating eggs full of mustard,' he said solemnly. 'Didn't stop him eating fresh ones, though.'

Methodically the spade entered the earth. 'I can see that bird now,' he said, and the clod moved forward. 'He ran round and round that pen, with his beak wide open, squarking summat dreadful for over an hour. Thought we'd killed him.'

The spade entered the earth again. 'He was panting summat horrible, and damn near drank his water pot dry by the time he'd finished.'

Another spadeful went forward. 'The old sod knew the difference between a good egg and a doctored one. Never touched another one, no matter how carefully my wife blew it, and filled it with mustard. Seems he could smell it.'

'How did you cure him, then?' I asked.

'Cut off the tip of his beak with my penknife,' He said, still digging. 'Beak's like a finger-nail, Cut it too short, and it's tender, I made it too sore to bash a hole in an egg, but not too sore to pick up food. We had to trim him up once a week, ever after, or he reverted.'

'I only wish I could trim the beak of that crow,' I said. 'I'd even settle for doing it with the gun, but I can never get near enough to hit it.'

'That's the point,' The Old Boy said, straightening up from his spade. 'You never will get near enough to hit it. You've got to be clever, to get near enough to a crow.'

'How do I do that, then?' I asked, reminding him that I had spent fruitless hours hiding in the bushes, waiting for that accursed bird.

'You hid in the wrong place,' he said simply. 'The bird knew you were there. What you've got to do is hide where he isn't looking for you.'

I must have looked suitably stupid. Hiding somewhere at random, in the hope that a crow would fly overhead, didn't seem a particularly bright idea.

'He's got a home to go to,' Walter explained, 'with a mate sitting on eggs or youngsters to feed. Those old crows always nest over there,' he said, pointing out into the distance, over the farm, 'in those trees up along the marsh. No matter which way he leaves here, he always circles round and comes in over the bottom of the four acre orchard.'

'Are you sure?' I said dubiously. The marsh stretched out for several miles, its cliff-like bank edges being lined with trees all the way.

'As sure as one ever can be,' he replied. 'Best time to get him is after supper, just before the light begins to fail. That's when that old bird will go home.'

I began to plan, working out in my memory which was the next free evening, when I could sit out at the far end of

83

the apple orchard for several hours, and wait for that crow to go home.

'I'll show you the best place to be,' he said and, to my surprise, stopped digging, cleaned his spade, and walked methodically up to his shed. His tools carefully cared for and put away, he closed the shed door, and I followed him down the drive, over the road to the farm, and up the track to the far end.

The cox's apple orchard was on a gentle slope, facing south, with the wooded marsh at the bottom, and shelter belts of trees to either side. A high hedge of elms protected the whole site from the north winds.

The apple trees themselves were growing in rows, in strips of bare earth, kept free from grass and weeds by the regular application of herbicides, but the wide roads between the bare strips were lush grass. Later this grass would be cut to provide a moisture-retaining mulch to force the growth of apples, but now it was verdant, lush, and nearly a foot high.

'Follow me,' The Old Boy ordered, and we set off into the trees. We seemed to be pursuing a very erratic path through the virgin grass, dodging in and out of the rows of trees. He turned round to face me. 'It's most important you come this way,' he said. 'If you go straight there, that old bird will see you coming.'

We proceeded on our way, alternating our steps alongside a few trees, then across and through a row or two, always walking down the slope, till finally we came to the far bottom corner. At the very bottom of the field was a steep bank. In prehistoric times, when the marsh had been the open sea, it had been the cliff edge. It ran the whole width of the field, ten or twenty yards wide, acutely angled, and covered in five-feet-high stinging nettles. They formed a dense, impenetrable barrier to anything larger than a rabbit, the needle hairs on the leaves bristling and distended with venom.

'Shouldn't like to walk through that lot,' I remarked idly. The chances of slipping down that steep bank seemed quite high.

We walked back up, twenty yards or so from the bank of vicious-looking nettles, and looked for a place to hide from the sharp eyes of that vigilant crow. Carefully the old man reconnoitred the site, and finally selected a spot just between two trees, but well into a row. 'You sit here, boy,' he said. 'That old crow 'll come down along that hedge here. You'll see him acomin', and if the first barrel don't get him, the second will.'

I could see what he meant. Provided that the crow followed the expected flight path, when standing up I had a clear view over the trees in all directions, more than adequate for two barrels of gunshot. Sitting still under the branches, now just beginning to bend earthwards under the weight of growing apples, I was to all intents and purposes invisible from every side.

Looking round, I was suddenly aware that the area around me had been well used by someone or something. In the next strip, there was a well-trodden path through the long grass, culminating in a small dell between the trees, where the grass had been totally flattened. Any cavorting animals or courting couples lying in this dell would be totally invisible from more than a few yards away.

I sat under the branches and watched. I had a clear view out into the sky, it was an extremely pleasant place, restful and relaxing. It was quiet, very quiet; the only sounds were a soporific background buzzing of multitudes of insects going about their business, and high above, a skyful of larks twittered at the edge of hearing.

Crow or no crow, it was a place where I could spend an hour or two recharging my emotional batteries, while I waited for it.

'Come on,' the old man said, and I heaved myself reluctantly to my feet. 'You be sure you're here and in position by half-six at the latest.'

We retraced our steps back up to the top of the orchard. Old Walter led the way. Halfway through the trees, he stopped, and pointed backwards to the path we had made in the verdant grass. 'You make sure you come this way again tonight,' he insisted. 'Waste of time if you're seen coming.'

I followed him to the top of the orchard, and we looked down the slope, over the tops of the apple trees, to the hidden spot at the bottom.

'Yes,' he said. 'That's a good place for you,' and turning away, we walked back down the path towards home. 'Don't you forget,' he insisted as we walked away. 'You've got to be there, unseen, before time.'

It was most uncharacteristic of him to insist I did or did not do anything. Usually he would drop the broadest hints, in the form of questions, like, 'Will you be cutting the grass tonight?' The admission that I had planned to do something else always made me feel very guilty, and generally resulted in him getting his own way.

I did not realise then that in this matter he had an ulterior motive, but he had quite persuaded me that tonight was the best time to do it. Mac would be on call.

My afternoon visits and evening surgery were uneventful; after a quick, early supper, I took my gun from its case and, putting a handful of cartridges into my pocket, walked slowly and quietly over the road, up the lane and across to the cox's orchard. Silently I retraced the path Old Walter and I had made through the grass earlier in the day. It was a glorious evening. The sun had really come out, and at this season of the longest day was warm and still high in the western sky. The insects, too, still murmured, but the larks had ceased to chatter to each other.

I sat in my appointed spot beneath the apple tree, the sun warm and comfortable on my face and bare arms, listening to the almost-silence, and staring up into the empty sky. According to Old Walter, there was still at least an hour to wait, and deep down I was still sceptical that the crow would come this way at all.

Warm and comfortable, with the sun shining into my face, my eyelids began to feel heavy and slowly closed. With a jerk, I opened them, and scanned the empty sky again. There was not even a lark. The heaviness entered my eyelids again. I wallowed in the luxury of the sensation, and although seemingly wide awake, could have been said to be asleep.

Something moved in the sky. I must have perceived a shadow through my closed lids, but it was only a pigeon passing over, high up, and utterly oblivious of my presence beneath. I watched it hurry across the sky, and with the sun still on my face, let my eyes become heavy again, and the warm indolence re-enter my soul.

After a while, suddenly, with a jerk that instantly had me fully alert, I became unconsciously aware that I was not alone. There was not a bird in the sky and, clutching my loaded gun, I searched for visible evidence of that sixth-sense awareness of the close proximity of another presence.

I could see nothing. Hear nothing. The hairs on the back of my neck began to prickle, and I could feel the pulse hammering in my chest. Cautiously I looked around. Nothing moved, there was no sound, but I knew there was something, or someone, nearby.

I waited, the adrenalin in my blood keeping me at full alert, as I scoured the sky for birds, and searched the grass stalks for the slightest movement – evidence of a rabbit, or perhaps a fox. There was nothing, every blade of grass was still. A good ten minutes passed, or it could have been half an hour. My eyes and ears repeatedly told me that I was alone, but I knew that somewhere, very near, was another human presence. Finally I heard it – a deep, solitary sigh – and the tall stalks at the edge of the little dell moved, one row of trees away, as a body rolled over.

I did not know who it was, or how they had got there. I was certain that there had been no one lying in the little dell when I had taken up my station under the trees, and I had definitely not heard or seen anyone come. Perplexed, I wondered what to do, vaguely resentful not only of the fact that whoever it was, was trespassing, but also knowing that their presence would probably ruin my intended ambush of the crow. Uncertain, I did nothing, and just sat there waiting.

The grass moved again. A hand appeared above the top of the stalks, a female hand, holding a bottle of suntan oil. Fascinated, I watched the other hand appear, take off the top of the bottle, and then open out to receive some of the bottle contents as they were shaken into it.

The hands subsided, and I listened hard for the sound of oil being massaged into flesh, but could not hear it.

After a while, the owner of the hands slowly sat up. It was Moira Jones. All that part of her that I could see was totally naked. The suntan so assiduously acquired did not stop at the top of the halter handkerchief, but continued on down her body. Her ample breasts were as brown as the rest of her. Slowly, and with obvious pleasure, she began gently to massage the oil into her breasts, raising an arm as she did so, as if to show them off. Eventually, she finished and lowered herself back, out of my sight, into the grass.

I sat there, wondering what to do. She could not possibly have known that I had watched her, and there seemed no point in announcing my presence as a Peeping Tom. While I dithered, she spoke, softly and endearingly, but not to me. Someone else was coming, quietly and furtively, from the bottom of the orchard, up the row of trees. I caught a glimpse between the leaves as he lay down beside her. It was not her solicitor's clerk husband, but Rupert, our new farm worker. He disappeared from view into the grass, to the accompaniment of muted giggles. They sat up again, and I watched her remove his shirt and anoint his chest

88

with oil. The giggles and cavorting continued as they played with the oil and each other. Bits of clothing appeared around the grass. It was definitely time for me to creep away. Somewhat shocked, I had no desire to witness any more of this adultery, but neither had I any great urge to let them know that they had been observed. I was just a little annoyed that they had spoiled the peace of my evening, and ruined any chance of getting that black, predatory crow.

Quietly, I started to stand up and move away; but there, up at the top of the orchard, quartering over it as he hunted, was that crow. I realised that it, too, had not seen me.

Half crouched, I froze. The crow continued to flap to and fro across the trees, while the soft rhythmic sounds of love behind me merged into the grass.

Unsuspecting, the crow searched on, slowly coming ever nearer as he moved back and forth, but still well out of range of my shotgun as I hid under the branches of the apple trees. The crow moved more over to the right. Out of the corner of my eye I was aware of passion in the dell. All I could see, as I followed the movement of the crow, was a bare backside, stark white and surprisingly spotty, rising rhythmically out of the grass.

The crow crossed the field; my eyes followed it, and I turned my back on the lovers from whom soft moaning sounds were now coming. The crow turned and retraced his steps, just that little bit nearer. A few more yards and it would be in range, but it turned back again.

I waited while it quartered the field again. As it approached, I could see that stark-white backside, now moving frenetically, and the moaning suddenly became very loud.

The crow floated agonisingly just out of range, but moving nearer. The noise increased. I felt the crow must hear it.

'Pssst,' I hissed angrily at them. 'Be quiet.'

The tone of the moaning lowered, but did not stop. The crow flapped a little nearer, and just as it was almost close enough, the noise increased.

'Shut up,' I hissed at them, a little louder.

This time they heard me. 'What the hell was that?' came an anxious whisper, and all movement stopped.

The world seemed to hang in suspense. The crow floated into range. Hurriedly, I threw up the gun, and fired.

I knew I had missed. The crow, seeing the naked bodies sitting up anxiously, had jinked wildly, and increased speed and height to fly over them. The second shot was pure reflex. The crow never knew what hit it and, dead in the air, its beak and wings hanging wildly down, it fell out of the sky, the momentum of its motion carrying it forward towards the occupants of the dell.

I was aware of them sitting up, naked and open-mouthed, as the dead crow hurtled towards them. She screamed as it thumped into the ground between them, a bloody mass of black feathers, open beak, flapping wings and claw-like feet.

They both scrambled to their feet and, grabbing wild handfuls of clothes, fled out of the dell, down the grass path. I heard them crashing, falling and crying, naked, down the stinging-nettle cliff. The contrast of his tight, spotty little white backside against her ample nut-brown one, was a vision that stayed in my mind as I heard them crashing away. They had not seen me, and had no idea who had fired the shots.

Silently, I emerged from beneath the tree and, unobserved, went to pick up my crow. I noticed his trousers and her handkerchief top still lying in the grass. I left them there, and headed up the path for home.

*   *   *

'Did you get it?' Ruth said, as I walked in through the door. 'I heard the shots.'

'Yes,' I replied, putting the gun on the table, and opened the cupboard to get out the cleaning rod.

'Where's the corpse, then?' she asked dubiously. 'I know you. If you'd really shot it, you'd have run home in triumph, shouting and waving it in the air.'

I told her about the courting couple.

'So that's why Old Walter was so insistent you went tonight,' she said. 'He knew they'd be there, and wanted you to catch them.'

'The cunning old devil,' I said. Then it hit me. 'The best part is still to come,' I told her. 'You remember Sylvester Jones, the solicitor's clerk, her husband, the fitness fanatic who insists on cycling at least ten miles every day?'

'Of course,' she replied. 'He's the one who wanted to take up taxidermy, and asked you to let him have the bodies of any ducks that died. You never did give him any, did you?'

'Well, no,' I replied. 'But Old Walter has been telling him of some incredible long-lost bridle ways that it's still possible to cycle along. I met him at the fruit farm entrance as I was coming out. Walter had drawn him a map of one that runs along the edge of the marsh, at the bottom of the cox's orchard, and he was just off to try it out.'

'You didn't let him go, did you?' she asked, aghast.

'No,' I said. 'I persuaded him to take the crow home and stuff it instead. He has a theory that if he stuffs it, and mounts it in an aggressive position in a glass case, placed on the island, it will keep other crows off the teal nests. I didn't disillusion him.'

'I've got some very good news,' she said. 'Old Walter came round soon after you'd gone. He thought he knew where we'd find that Baikal teal nest. She's sitting on it. The crow didn't get it after all.'

8

Paperwork is tedious, particularly that part of it that relates to being taxed.

Agricultural wages boards, PAYE, the outputs and inputs of VAT, Apple and Pear Development Councils and Agricultural Census Boards, all demanded time, money and the rectification of mistakes. The common-or-garden taxman insisted on his rights, and prompt replies to his demands for Schedule D, Schedule E, and others that I didn't understand.

As a secretary, Ruth was hopeless. She refused even to acknowledge the existence of such unpleasant persons.

Letters from them all accumulated in heaps on the sideboard in the kitchen, buried underneath piles of old newspapers, junk mail, and other items that needed attention, like socks queueing up to be mended. Bills she put in an enormous paper-clip hanging behind the back door. Beneath it waited the kitchen waste bin.

Periodically the clip became so full that it sprang open, showering the papers and envelopes all over the floor.

If the lid of the bin happened to be open at the time, too bad. Those that fell in, stayed there.

Some merchants, who used those slippery brown envelopes with see-through address windows, persistently lost all chance of payment that month, simply because their envelopes were too slippery to stay in the clip.

It seemed that every time I sat down to deal with all that paper, something cropped up. A baby stuck in deep transverse arrest and needing urgent forceps delivery; someone having a heart attack; next door's cattle eating the strawberries; so-called automatic watering systems for all those ducks breaking down; someone demanding a new incubator; or perhaps a child's school sports day which I had overlooked.

There came to be a jinx on it. To start gathering the paper was the signal for the phone to ring. It was far easier, and less stressful, to leave it to accumulate.

After a while, the sheer volume of all that paper waiting to be processed, combined with the angry demands from unpaid creditors, vociferous taxmen, and the heartfelt cries of 'Get it out of my kitchen', began to affect my health.

Something had to be done, but I had no idea what.

The solution had lain under my nose for months. His name was Edmund Franklin, and it wasn't until he had volunteered his services that I saw that he was the answer to all our problems.

As a patient, I had known him for years. He was an infrequent attender at the surgery. About the time that I had agreed to buy the fruit farm, he had been taken ill with abdominal pain. The cause had not been instantly obvious, so I had called to see him several times, to assess progress. During the course of various examinations, I had excitedly told him all about my purchase and asked his advice on selling all the produce.

Other than his pain, he did not mention his problems to me. He was the manager, and local director, of a national wholesaling and retail concern.

His pain puzzled me. It was not caused by any of the usual more common disorders; so, after consultation with our local surgeon, I arranged for his admission to Norwich. It took them several weeks to get to the bottom of it and perform the necessary operation.

Edmund Franklin eventually returned home, cured but very weak, and in need of prolonged convalescence.

During this period of his illness, a bigger multinational

concern took over his national employers. They decided to rationalise their operations and amalgamate Edmund's branch with another.

In the normal course of events, Edmund Franklin would automatically have assumed managership of both branches, but he was in hospital, undergoing major surgery. Feeling at that time extremely low, and somewhat overtaken by events, he offered to stand down in favour of his opposite number, the manager of the other, smaller branch. In return, the company would pay him his full pension and allow him to keep his company car.

This was readily agreed; so, at the early age of sixty, Edmund resigned, confidently assuming that he had made adequate arrangements for his financial future.

He was extremely distressed to discover that his opposite number, in his new capacity as manager and local director, declined to implement the agreement.

Edmund's full pension, deemed by himself and his old company to be what he would have been entitled to, had he remained working to retirement age, was deemed by his ex-colleague, on behalf of the new company, to be the legal minimum of repayment of contributions: an inadequate pittance.

As for the car: 'What car?' he was asked. It had to be sold at full price. Edmund could purchase it if he wished.

In vain did Edmund appeal to the new multinational.

'A purely local matter,' they told him. 'It is not our policy to overrule the first decision of a new local director.'

Sad, disillusioned, and remarkably philosophical, Edmund Franklin attended the surgery, and offered to sort out my paperwork.

It was an offer I gratefully received.

Cash flows, budgets, wages, PAYE – they were all meat and drink to him. Agricultural census forms, Apple and Pear Development Council levies – they all flashed across his desk with gratifying speed.

It took him a matter of weeks to sort out all the existing problems. During those weeks his health improved dramatically: so much so that, each morning, before I set off to the surgery, Edmund came to open the post and have it dealt with before I could escape to work. He was so keen that he almost lay in ambush for the postman, as this good worthy came up the drive.

He also made me aware of the old maxim that any fool can produce it. The difficult part is selling it.

He conferred for hours with Frank, extracting facts, like forty tons of strawberries to be sold in July. He spent hours on the phone to wholesale fruit merchants, and came to the conclusion that they were a load of parasitic vultures, with only their own profits at heart. Fruit farmers were merely the carrion on which they fed.

His answer was Pick Your Own.

'I shall need some help,' he said diffidently. Edmund was exceedingly conscious not only of his own straitened financial circumstances, but also of mine. Little items, like not taking his own agreed salary until the money for the strawberries was in, he didn't bother me with.

He explained his strategy. It was very simple: inform as many people as possible of their opportunity to pick their own strawberries, in the week before we opened.

It sounded simple, but there was a great deal of work involved. Posters had to be printed and displayed. He had ideas of advertising not only in the paper, but on the buses, in the local cinemas, even on TV.

Having done his advertising, the next stage was organising the people, setting up the till points, weighing the fruit, and taking the money.

'At peak periods,' he said, 'if it all works out, we shall need at least five people manning the stalls.'

'Do you know such people?' I asked him. 'People who can be trusted with all that money, who are available to work for such a short summer season?'

'Oh, yes,' he said casually. Edmund had a very wide

circle of friends, many of whom were like himself – ex-managerial, retired, active, and not averse to earning an honest shilling.

The first one he produced was Bob Cutter. Bob was a natural manic depressive. I knew him as a patient of Mac's, and he had consulted me on occasion about his medication. He took a regular dose of Lithium, which kept him more or less on the straight and narrow. Every few months he needed a blood test, to check that the level of Lithium in his body was neither too much nor too little.

When he was depressed, he was bad, suicidal and morose. The Lithium kept at bay the very worst of his depression, but when the natural cycle of the disorder lifted him out of depression into the manic phase, Bob went over the top with bonhomie.

For most of the time he was somewhere between the two, on a more or less even keel.

He had spent his working life in a bank. His natural ability should have taken him to the very top, but his spells of depression had severely hampered his promotion. When he was manic, he had been known to lend out the bank's money to the most undeserving causes, with such reckless abandon that the bank had demoted him to a position where he was only able to count it, not lend it out.

He had hated the bank all his life. The opportunity to take an early discharge, and retire on medical grounds, had rejuvenated his spirit. It was sometimes difficult to tell if he was merely exceptionally pleased with life, or going manic again.

Joy was in his heart, a song on his lips, as he toured the town and countryside, slapping posters on any wall that stayed still, and any bus that moved. Cafés, restaurants, shops, were all blessed with a dop of paste, and a fruit farm poster. I was acutely embarrassed at some of the places he chose for them, passing by on the other side, pretending that they weren't mine.

But it worked. An awful lot of people knew that we would be opening for Pick Your Own.

The second helper that Edmund pressganged was Joe Silverman. Joe was the very opposite of Bob – quiet, shy, unobtrusive, and an engineer.

Joe was a diesel engine expert, a designer and maker of motor yachts. Trained at one of the famous Lowestoft shipyards, he had been chief engineer on the yacht of an American-Jewish margarine magnate, stuck in the Mediterranean, when the Germans had moved into the South of France.

He had spent a very uncomfortable war. He did not talk about it – in fact he talked very little – but he loved engines.

Edmund had summoned him out of a comfortable retirement to be chief maintenance mechanic.

Frank directed the machinery, but refused to drive it. Young Rupert did the driving, under Frank's eagle eye, but he had no mechanical sense. When even I could hear the screams of tortured metal being pushed beyond its limits, and could feel the inevitable wreckage coming on, Rupert could only sense it wasn't working, and opened throttles to put in more power.

The breakdown rates were appalling, particularly as most of the malfunctions were caused by a lack of oil and grease, a basic maintenance that neither Frank nor Rupert was capable of understanding.

Edmund summoned Joe to quietly sort them out.

He was very successful. It was something to do with the expression on his face, when they broke something twice. He continued to say very little.

The great day arrived. The strawberries were ripe, the stalls, with tills and scales ready, and manned by a gang of eager old age pensioners, stood waiting.

Bob and Edmund paced up and down the car parking area, ropes and marshalling sticks at the ready.

It was eight o'clock on a Sunday morning. Already a

queue of cars had formed in the road outside. I flung open the gates. The cars rolled in.

By lunchtime we had handled two thousand cars, sold four tons of strawberries, and run out of ripe fruit.

The problems of success had hardly begun.

9

The old age pensioners had succeeded beyond their (and my) wildest dreams. Not only had Bob Cutter covered the surrounding area with posters, but Edmund had managed to persuade the editor of the local paper, another friend of his, that our venture was extremely newsworthy. He gave us full coverage, with a front page picture of Ruth and the children pretending to pick green strawberries.

It was a good picture, taken by myself, and pinched from the family album as I was about to stick it in.

He also had it made into a slide for projection, with the interval ice cream, in every cinema within a thirty-mile radius.

I had grave doubts when Bob told me that he had also opened negotiations with the advertising people at Anglia Television. He said they had told him that they were, for some reason, short of advertisers for the 'ten second' slots just before they closed down for the night.

It seemed to Bob that the sum of money they quoted for flashing Ruth's picture at the late night viewers, with the exhortation to come and join her picking strawberries, was very reasonable.

Time, he said, late at night, on Mondays, was very cheap. Could he have my authority to book one single flash on a Monday night?

Reluctantly, I agreed.

I don't know what went wrong: it must have been something to do with the World Cup running concurrently with our strawberry crop.

They failed to show our advertisement at the time we had booked. Bob went puce, and shouted at some poor girl on the other end of the telephone, but couldn't get past her.

Tuesday night, we all sat up to watch, but again no advert appeared.

Wednesday, Thursday and Friday were equally blank. I began to think that Bob had not only gone manic, but developed delusions of grandeur as well, even thinking of putting out television adverts. I presumed that the whole thing had been a non-starter.

On Saturday afternoon, the last day before we opened the gates for Pick Your Own strawberries, the family settled down to watch the World Cup Final. As the teams ran out onto the field, there was a technical hitch in transmission.

The television engineers filled the thirty-second gap with the first advertisement to hand, a picture of Ruth and the children picking strawberries. All those people about to watch the World Cup, from Lincolnshire to North London via the East Midlands, were exhorted to come and join her picking strawberries on our fruit farm.

It was small wonder that our car park was full. Bob was triumphant, really over the top – it was the high point of his manic phase. Thereafter, he sank slowly into depression, not to come up again until it was time for the apples.

Edmund's advertisements requested everyone to bring their own containers. Assuming that a lot of people, seeing the signs on the road, would call on the spur of the moment, he had also bought a thousand baskets, to be sold to the public at cost. By mid-day on that first Sunday, he had sold out.

Many and varied were the containers that came to be filled with strawberries, and it soon became very apparent that each one had to be weighed empty, before the picking started. Two identical old ladies, elegantly bearing two identical bowls, filled both bowls to capacity, with an equal volume of strawberries. One bowl weighed seven pounds more than than the other.

Every picker was exhorted to memorise the exact weight of their bowls, lest they have to pay for the weight of them in strawberries. Very very few failed to do so. Until he became too depressed even to turn up, Bob was very adept at persuading old ladies and the weights of their bowls not to get separated.

Some containers beat us. The classic was a new yellow dustbin. About twenty people set to, with gusto, to fill it with strawberries.

'The ones at the bottom will get squashed to pulp,' I told them with some horror. 'They'll be useless, just juice.'

'So what?' they shrugged.

'I'll give you the baskets,' I pleaded, 'if you're going to pick that quantity. I can't bear the thought of all that lovely fruit being squashed and ruined.'

'No problem,' they said. 'We're only going to make wine with it anyway.'

Full, that dustbin was too heavy to carry. We had to fetch the tractor and buckrake to get it off the field and loaded into their car. We agreed to one hundredweight of fruit – no scales of ours could possibly weigh it – but in all probability it was twice that. Since they never came back, we never heard how the wine came out, but I took a photograph of the full dustbin in the field, awaiting transport.

Inevitably, there were thieves. Peter the policeman set up watch and caught a surprising number of people creeping through the hedge onto the road, with containers of fruit unpaid for. They went off in convoys of police cars to the station, to make statements. Peter made their departure very ostentatious. The word soon spread, especially when the magistrates fined the first offenders twenty pounds each.

Every Monday morning, at exactly five minutes to ten, Edmund would finish cashing up and set off to the bank, with several thousand pounds, in used notes, in a plastic shopping bag. In vain did I plead with him to vary his routine, lest he be observed and robbed. It was not until Peter the policeman read him the riot act that he was persuaded to let another person, in another car, by a different route, to perhaps another bank, at a different time of day, take the money in.

That first summer was a mad rush through the successively ripening crops. As Bob became more morose and depressed, he came only on occasions. We all knew it was only a matter of time before he came out of it; I gave him full doses of antidepressants, and we all waited. His friends had seen him through it too often before to be worried.

His place in the rota was taken by Roy and Mary, recently retired publicans. Although they had looked forward for years to their retirement, they found the reality very lonely. They missed the company more than they cared to say. Roy cheerfully admitted he would have paid to come to work, to stand out in the sunshine and meet all his old friends again.

The fact that his job had been taken over so effectively made Bob even more depressed. I reassured him again and again that there was room for all of them.

'There's two parts to this depression. It's a chemical thing,' he told me, one day when I had called to see him at his home. 'Something inside me makes this stuff that causes the depression, and I can feel it building up.'

'How do you mean?' I asked.

'Two parts, like I said. The first part loads the gun, the second pulls the trigger.'

'Go on,' I said.

'Something, some process inside me, makes this chemical. I know it's going on, building up, but I can't stop it, can't control it.'

He paused, sorting out the right words to explain.

'When the gun's loaded, something pulls the trigger, releasing all that chemical into my blood. I can feel it happening. Somebody says something, somebody does something, something goes wrong, and wham – out it all comes.'

He looked at me.

'I can feel it happen, like a waterfall flowing down inside me. I cry like a baby, "No, please, stop it!" but it comes on just the same, and I can feel myself going down that black hole of depression all over again, and I can't get out.'

'I know,' I said. 'Medically it's coming to be accepted that depression is a chemical thing, but we don't know enough about it.'

'I know all about it,' he said bitterly. 'Once that stuff's all in my blood, it takes weeks to be removed. All I want is to be left alone, to die quietly. And then, as it starts to clear, I know that more is forming. Someone is going to say something, do something, and pull the trigger all over again.'

'Do you think the pills help?'

'A little,' he admitted. 'That depression is just like a deep hole. It's dark, and very lonely down there. You can't talk to anybody. I find loud music is the only thing that holds me – loud classical music; it drowns out all those morbid thoughts that go round and round, and round again.

'Yes, the pills help. The hole isn't quite so deep and dark, but still the effort to get out, and get above the effects of that chemical, whatever it is, is difficult; and just when you can see out of it, and there's light at the top, someone says something, something happens, it pulls the trigger on a fresh lot, and down you go to the bottom of the hole again.'

'And when you come out of the depressive phase again?'

'That stuff's just not being made. People can pull my trigger as much as they like, the gun's just not loaded. I know when I'm getting out of it: the black hole is not so deep, and I'm only in it for a few days when the trigger's pulled.'

Over the month of August he slowly recovered. The August gap, Edmund called it. We had nothing to sell. We had even sold our crop of potatoes.

The potatoes had been grown, at Frank's suggestion, on part of a field doing nothing that spring. He thought the crop would clean some of the weeds out of it.

Many of our neighbours grow potatoes. As a favour, I had persuaded one of them, young William, to plant our two acres when he was planting his own first earlies. His massive machinery had made a few passes up and down and, in the slight interval between tea and supper, had done the job.

I had given no thought as to how they would be harvested. William had contract-sold his to the canners. Contractors had descended on his fields and whisked his potatoes away. No contractor would bother with my small two acre bit.

Under Frank's direction, Rupert had sprayed them for weeds and blight, and we had a fine crop.

'How do we sell them?' I had asked Edmund.

'Dig Your Own,' he had replied dubiously, adding that he had better put an advertisement in the paper, telling all those interested in the taste of fresh potatoes, straight from the ground, to bring their own forks.

The novelty of the idea appealed.

It was a glorious Sunday morning. The sun shone, barely a cloud in the sky, and the car park was full of people, dressed for the summer. Holidaymakers were in profusion, in summer dresses, bare legs and high-heeled shoes. A surprising number had come with their garden forks, and strode purposefully to the potatoes. Some were forkless, but set off just the same. Others were armed with bits of wood or steel bars, and not a few had brought table forks, with which they attacked the ground.

We had never seen anything like it. They spread out all over the field, like goldminers staking a claim, and frantically began to dig. There is something about potatoes in a field, somewhat akin, I should imagine, to gold in a mine. As long as the digger thinks that there is another potato under his fork, he will keep digging.

Rupert was recruited to ferry the tractor and cart to and fro, hauling the heavy sacks to the scales in the car park to be weighed. Every meal sack that had once held duck food was gathered up, turned inside out, and filled with spuds.

Crowds attract more people. All kinds of folk, who had merely come out on a lovely summer afternoon, dressed in their best, found themselves scrabbling in the earth, with long red fingernails, for potatoes.

By the end of the second weekend of such treatment, the field was in a complete mess. The potato miners had dug in a very sporadic manner, in places very deep, in others not at all. The still growing tops were trampled into the earth. It was total chaos, and although many novices could now find no potatoes, over half the crop still lay in the ground.

William was summoned to give advice and help and, if possible, to lend his potato harvester to get the rest out.

'Never seen anything like it,' he repeated over and over again, as he watched an elegant housewife, dressed in a very smart two-piece suit, with matching white handbag and gloves laid carefully on the earth beside her, lever into the baulk of the row with a nailfile, and in triumph gather up a small bag of new potatoes.

'My machine would be no good here,' he said at last. 'It's too big. It needs eight people to work it, and by the time we'd got them all here, it would be time to go home. Besides, mine puts the spuds straight into a bag; your people here want to pick them up off the earth. What you want is one of the oldfashioned single row spinners, that just spins the potatoes out and leaves them lying on the ground.'

'Have you got one?' I asked hopefully.

'No,' he said, 'but I can ring round. Someone's bound to have one lying up under a hedge somewhere.'

Someone did. It was ours if we could take it away. No payment, it would tidy the hedge up.

I took Rupert and Joe and a tractor over to fetch it. It had lain deep in a nettle bed for years. Through it and over it grew inch-thick brambles, hawthorn suckers and seedling sycamores. It took them most of an afternoon to free it. Rupert showed a surprising distaste for stinging nettles.

Joe oiled it and greased it, freed its various rusted joints with heat and solvents, and finally pronounced it fit to travel. Very gingerly Rupert brought it home behind his tractor.

He had been threatened by Joe that if he broke it, due to carelessness or non-attention, the only job that he, Rupert, would be fit for after Joe had finished with him, would be a choirboy in the treble section of the Vatican choir. Rupert was very careful.

Together they made it functional, freeing, oiling, greasing and welding.

The first operational trial run was a triumph. Rupert drove the tractor very carefully up the first row. Behind him, clanking, groaning and spinning, the metal arms flailed round, leaving a neat row of rotavated earth, on top of which lay the potatoes.

The digging public, seeing those exposed tubers, ran for them. Potatoes which, in the cold light of a greengrocer's shop, would have been rejected on grounds of size, shape or damage, were eagerly seized before someone else got them first.

Like seagulls following a plough, they followed Rupert. Some people, suddenly realising that there were no more potatoes under their feet, ran, past all those who were busy picking up, to the back of the tractor where more new ones, freshly exposed, were waiting.

We watched, spellbound, while the whole cavalcade passed slowly across the field.

Rupert, aware of the dignity of his position, and the ridiculous greed of the scrabbling crowd behind him, rode high on his tractor, a fixed grin on his face, a grin that stretched from ear to ear. When he reached the end of the field, he stopped, allowed the crowd to clear what he had dug up, and then, as they poised to pounce, he returned back up the next row.

So it went on all that Sunday afternoon.

Within a very short space of time, we had run out of potatoes and had to start buying them in from our neighbours, in sacks. They sold just as well. The demand for fresh produce seemed insatiable.

All during August, Edmund bought in potatoes, runner beans, cauliflowers – anything he could get his hands on – so that we should have something to sell, while we waited for the apples to ripen, and for Bob to rise up out of his depressive phase.

There was no doubt that the Lithium and the other antidepressants definitely did shorten his depressive cycle, and prevent him from going too far down into his deep, dark hole.

He started reappearing again at the farm. We could tell his mood. Always, as his depression lifted, whatever the weather, he wore a hat. When really depressed, he didn't bother. As he became more manic and expansive, the size of his hats increased. When really over the top, he preferred an old Australian bush hat.

We knew he was on the mend when he appeared one morning, wearing his blue French beret. He had come to supervise the apple harvest.

Frank was somewhat apprehensive about letting the public loose on his apple crop.

'They'll knock down and damage far more than they pick,' he asserted.

In the large orchard he was indubitably right: they wandered about, picking an apple here and another there; but if we confined them to a much smaller space, the same greed that was so apparent on the potato field showed itself again. Some of them almost came to blows over the apples they had knocked off in scrambling for them while they were still on the tree.

It soon became apparent that there was no way the public would pick the whole apple crop off the trees. The bulk would have to be picked, and stored in the barn.

After two or three weeks into the apple season, Bob was noted to be wearing his Austrian Tyrol hat, with feather.

We had all agreed that we must have the apples sold by Christmas. Beyond that date, not having been cold-stored, they would be past their best.

Bob and Edmund eyed the pile of apples still in the barn, divided it by the number of days left, and came up with the answer that they weren't going to do it. They had set out two rows of apples boxes, thirty pounds in each box, and twenty or so boxes in a row, and invited the public to choose their own.

When two boxes became half empty, they tipped one into the other, and brought out a fresh box.

A lot of apples were going, but not enough.

'We need a loss leader, to bring them in,' Bob stated, after he'd once again done his poster round, and deemed that there still weren't enough people buying apples.

'What about some of Old George's pot plants?' I suggested. 'That might help.'

It was agreed to try it. I fetched a carful on an experimental basis, and soon had to go back for more. It all helped, but it was not enough.

By now, Bob had moved up to his deerstalker. This had a very large brim over his eyes, and an even bigger one over the back of his neck.

'Christmas trees,' he exclaimed suddenly. 'Christmas trees. Everyone wants a Christmas tree.' Off he went to find out where and how to purchase Christmas trees.

I should have known, I should have seen. He returned, wearing his Australian bush hat, but I was busy, and Mac was on his annual golfing holiday; so unrestrained, whistling a happy tune, his depression all behind him, and Edmund as blissfully ignorant as I was, Bob went off again, with full authority to purchase Christmas trees.

It was later, much later, before I really discovered what had happened. Bob had applied a little elementary logic to the problem. My hair would have turned white, had I known what he was doing.

Christmas trees come from the Forestry Commission. He had phoned the Forestry Commission, found out just where they were cutting Christmas trees, and ascertained their ultimate destination.

He had then made a trip to the offices of the various plantations, bought the lot, and arranged for them to be shipped to the fruit farm.

His next step was to scour all the adverts in the various trade papers, and find out which private growers were advertising. He personally visited as many as he could, bought their entire output, and again arranged transport to the fruit farm.

His final coup had been to hear of a ship coming in to Yarmouth from Belgium, laden with Christmas trees. To his everlasting regret, most of her cargo was already sold and on its way to Birmingham, but the remainder he bought on the dock.

It was at this point that he brought the bills to Edmund, asking for prompt payment.

Edmund, almost in heart failure, started ringing round all those wholesalers whom he had described so recently as vultures, feeding on the carrion of the bodies of small fruit growers, to see if he could sell them some Christmas trees.

Bob had beaten him to it. They all knew that the fruit farm had the total monopoly of Christmas trees for virtually the whole of East Anglia. Quite happily they ordered, with a respectable profit on each tree. Just normal business to them.

Poor Edmund spent a whole sleepless week organising lorries, ferrying Christmas trees he'd never seen, to parts of the country he'd never been to.

If there had been room on his head, Bob would have worn two Australian bush hats. Just when Edmund thought that, thankfully, he had found customers for every tree, Bob was contacted by a very distressed vicar, who had filled his twenty acres of glebe land with Christmas trees. For five years he had lovingly tended them, weeded them, and brought them on to perfection for this Christmas.

The poor man had cut them all down, only to find that he had no market for them. Bob and Edmund between them had pinched his customers. He had appealed to Bob's better Christian nature. Bob had bought the lot, without telling us, and had them shipped to the farm.

The high pressure selling had to start all over again. Fortunately for us, there was a provident last-minute shortage of Christmas trees that year.

In the remaining few days before Christmas, that enormous stack of trees magically shrank. Bob and his gang of willing pensioners arranged them into long rows, big ones at one end, little ones at the other.

They sold them by the foot, and the apples with them. They even sold the last two trees, two poor broken specimens tied together to make one, to a desperate passer-by.

There were no trees, no plants and virtually no apples left, when they closed the farm for Christmas.

I had no idea what they'd done, until the cheques for these mind-boggling sums of money were presented to me for signature; but by that time, they'd sold the trees and the money for them was in the bank.

The friendly bank manager was exceedingly pleased with their efforts. I just sat shaking, thinking of what could have gone wrong. Edmund had aged ten years. Bob was still supermanic, and dreaming dreams of growing bananas in the spring.

After Christmas, Bob started to go depressive again – slowly, imperceptibly at first, back into his private black hole. Mac and I raised the doses of his medication, to almost over the safety limits. This controlled his descent into depression much more effectively, and, afterwards, his rise into mania as well.

He agreed with us that although it was safer and quieter, life was far less exciting. We waited for the spring, to see whether, in his new controlled moods, he would have forgotten all about bananas.

10

Old men forget, I reminded myself as I sat down once again by his bedside.

'Ask old Uncle Tom,' I had been told so often in my enquiries. 'He's the one who knows all the family history.'

And now I had Uncle Tom all to myself, and I could ask him all the questions I wanted.

'Ah, you mean Arthur,' he said, just like all the others, as I settled down to hear the story. 'Don't really talk about him a lot. He's the one who went off to be a coachman in a nunnery.'

'I know,' I replied. 'Tell me about him.'

The old man lying in the bed rested his head more firmly into his pillows, and closed his eyes.

'They put him in the wall in Godley,' he said finally, and that for him was the end of the conversation.

He had told me no more and no less than every other member of his family.

It was a big family. The grand old patriarch had come down from somewhere up north, in the great migration of Cumbrian farmers into East Anglia in the 1850s. He had not been a farmer, however, but an agricultural labourer, desperately poor, with an insatiable thirst for knowledge. In another age, he might well have become a professor of botany, but having a wife and family to support, he had grabbed at the priorities, at pennies.

On a small plot of land, working non-stop day and night, he had produced anything and everything that he could sell, ultimately coming to specialise in tomatoes, chrysanthemums and cress.

The first greenhouse he built had been very modest, a

crude structure on the side wall of the agricultural worker's cottage that he had rented. In this, he grew the first tomatoes in the area. With sheer hard work he became prosperous, and over the ensuing years fathered nine sons and one daughter. Old Uncle Tom was one of the younger sons, and the mysterious Arthur had been the eldest, a youth who had hated greenhouses, had apparently been allergic to tomatoes, and had run off to become a coachman in a nunnery.

Rumours abounded about the life he had led, but no one seemed to know anything definite, except that he had made the most of it. 'Like a coachman in a nunnery' was a phrase used to describe any situation of pleasure or leisure and, with a knowing wink, covered anything from extreme sexual frustration to gross debauchery.

I became quite determined to gather from the family more about this famous uncle of theirs, but none of them seemed to know much about him.

'You'll have to ask Uncle Tom,' they all said with a laugh. 'He's the only one who really knows.'

But Uncle Tom wasn't telling. Bit by bit, I extracted much of the family history from the old man, as he lay in his bed, all the time hoping that he would eventually tell me about his brother Arthur.

'In those days,' he reminisced, 'a box of tomatoes paid a man's wages for a week. Two boxes paid the foreman. They had to work for it, too.'

Tom was now almost ninety, his mind as sharp as ever, but he had 'gone off his legs'. This had happened relatively suddenly, due to a combination of arthritis of the hips and knees, combined with the insidious heart failure of age, and hardening of his main arteries.

He had spent his life in the greenhouses his father had built, perpetuating the methods of his father. It never crossed his mind to change these methods, or think of any innovations. The crops he grew were top quality, and he had earned a good living.

113

As he had aged, so had his greenhouses, and as he had disintegrated, so had they; so that now, as he lay in his bed, his houses fell into unusable decay. But he was content, he had followed the example of his father, and worked right up to the last.

When in the right mood, he was a fund of reminiscence. He knew that in this modern age of mechanisation his houses were useless. He told me many times that they were designed entirely for hand work, and even unskilled labour needed paying more than the equivalent of a box of tomatoes a week. They had lasted out his need of them, and for that he was grateful.

Sometimes I felt that he was also grateful for an excuse for stopping work, that would have satisfied his father. The price of tomatoes had steadily fallen relative to the cost of his method of producing them. His father would have understood that there was no point in working for the sake of it, just to lose money. He thus did not feel as guilty as he should, just lying in bed and sleeping all day. I had a suspicion that the 'going off his legs' was probably as much mental as physical. But then, at his age, he was entitled to a bit of peace, and I did not bother him with physiotherapy and modern gadgetry. For most of my visits, we just sat and talked.

The memory of his father was still revered. He told me of the prodigious efforts that were needed, at the height of his father's activities, to keep the greenhouses warm and the temperature controlled. Stoking the boilers and altering the ventilators was a full-time job in itself.

He told me of the regular whole wagonloads of coal that would be brought to Leapton Station, and of how it was all loaded by shovel onto the farm carts, and of how the horses pulled it, half a ton at a time, to the heap outside the boiler room. 'Four boxes of tomatoes bought a ton of coal,' he said. 'We needed two whole wagons a winter.'

Another special horse and cart were kept to take the

produce to the station, where it was loaded and shipped straight to London. 'Couldn't risk getting it dirty from the coal,' he said. 'Father had a reputation to keep up. Book-mad he was; he was always sending to London for books, and the books always came back in the tomato cart. They were all books by professors telling him how to grow various things. Do you know,' he said, staring up at me out of his bed, 'he paid six guineas for a book on how to grow cucumbers, and that at a time when a good man earned half a crown a week.'

'Did he really?' I said, and the old man continued, 'We went without a lot of things to pay for that book.'

After a pause, he went on. 'It was worth it, though. Do you know, Father set all the family up in a farm each, out of those greenhouses. It was cress for Christmas, lettuces for Easter, tomatoes and cucumbers all summer, and chrysanths all autumn. I was the only one who stayed at home, all the others went off to become farmers.'

'Even Arthur?' I asked.

'Oh no, not him. He went off to be a coachman in a nunnery, you know. They put him in the wall at Godley.'

It became very frustrating trying to get more out of him. He was the last of the line. I listened innumerable times to the stories of the coal and the tomatoes, and he thoroughly enjoyed telling me all about them all over again, but never could I get him to tell me more about his brother Arthur, the nunnery, and the wall at Godley.

One morning, the family sent for me. Old Uncle Tom had passed peacefully away in his sleep. He lay in bed, quite stiff with rigor mortis, just as if fast asleep, with a small smile of contentment on his already rigid face. They all agreed that he had had a good life, and now, at last, they could bulldoze all those awful decrepit old greenhouses away, and put up some new modern ones more suited to their needs.

Uncle Tom had never married, and since his father's

115

death had lived alone. Despite the devoted attentions of the many sisters-in-law, and their even more devoted daughters, the house remained a museum to the time of the original patriarch. It was, in estate agents' terms, in need of renovation. Idly, I wondered just which of the family would take it on, or if it would be sold.

Several months drifted by, during which I had no cause or need to think of the old man, or his house; so it was with some considerable surprise that I heard a new patient one evening surgery give his address as old Tom's cottage.

I just assumed that they had sold or rented it to him, but did not bother to ask. The newcomer was a mild-mannered bachelor from Glasgow, who informed me that he had migrated south to find work, there being none in his home town. Middle-aged, and ordinary in every sense of the word, his sole purpose in coming to see me was to register as a patient.

He assured me that he was in very good health. His only problem was unemployment, and he soon intended to sort that out.

The cottage did not undergo a revolution under his tenancy. To the curious passer-by, such as myself, it seemed that old Tom was still living there. All the old greenhouses, with the exception of the one actually leaning against the house, had been swept away and tidied up before he had moved in.

All that remained of them was a large hole in the ground, a hole that still held the rusty remains of the enormous old boiler. The sides of the hole were the old concrete walls of the boilerhouse, but the roof had fallen in. Brambles and stinging nettles grew out of the steps leading down to it. The family, having erected new, modern glasshouses some distance away, seemed to confirm my belief that they had disposed of the old residence when, after the grand clear-up, a new fence appeared, limiting the old cottage garden to a fraction of its former size.

Desultory, amateur patches of cultivation appeared within the boundaries of the new garden, and became covered with weeds again. The efforts of the new Scottish tenant were more reminiscent of the primitive slash and burn agriculture as practised by nomads of a tropical rain forest, than the serious work of a born horticulturist.

He tried – in spasms – he tried hard, but his bursts of enthusiasm were not matched by his knowledge and skill. His crops withered, while his weeds flourished. I gathered that he had not had a great deal of success in finding employment, either.

The second time I met the new tenant was late one glorious summer's afternoon. One of the smaller female members of the old family, aged about seven, came cycling up the drive to me in the garden.

'It's Mr McIntyre,' she said, utterly unconcerned at his predicament. 'He's fell down the old boiler hole, and can't get out.'

'Is he hurt?' I asked, turning off the motor mower, in the middle of the half-cut lawn.

'Dunno,' she replied. 'All he said was to ask you to come.'

'How long's he been there?' I asked anxiously. Holding the handlebars of her bike, she shrugged her shoulders. 'Didn't say.' Delicately she turned her bike round in the drive, and sat on the saddle.

'Sounded as if he was drunk again,' she said completely disinterestedly, and, pushing on the pedals of her bike, ambled off down the drive.

To her, there was obviously no urgency in the message. It was routine errand, like being sent to the village shop, so ordinary as to be beyond interest.

One would have expected that an accident, with some-one stuck in a hole, would be high drama. Thinking that I had better treat it as such, I left the mower in the middle of the lawn, leaped into my car, and drove to old Tom's cottage.

117

Mr McIntyre was indeed down in the old boiler hole. He was seated quite comfortably on the rusty remains, smoking his pipe. Clouds of dirty grey-black smoke arose out of the hole. The smell was quite revolting, more like burning pig manure than tobacco, with just a hint of smouldering rubber. He seemed very content.

It was obvious how he had come to be in the hole. Some half-cut nettles and a broken scythe lay on the top of the steps, while the flattened vegetation, pointing down hill, marked his sudden flailing path down the steps.

'Good evening,' he said cheerfully, looking up through his cloud of smoke.

I peered down at him. 'Are you all right?' I asked.

'Well, yes and no,' he said affably, in his soft Scottish accent. 'Ye wouldna be the doctor, would ye?'

I agreed that indeed I was, and that I had also come at high speed at his summons. It seemed strange that he didn't recognise me. Doctors, seeing so many people in the course of their day, often forget faces and names, but most people, seeing so few doctors in the course of theirs, usually remember the name and face of the man they consulted with their troubles.

'Something's wrong with my eyes tonight,' he said, rubbing them.

The little girl was right. His speech, through the thick Glaswegian accent, did sound a trifle slurred and slow, as if he had been drinking.

'It's ma ankle,' he said. 'Canna stand on it. I think the rest of me's awright.'

Gingerly, I walked down the steps into the old boiler-room, picking my way carefully over and through the flattened nettles and trailing brambles, to where he was seated on the boiler. His ankle was swollen and painful, but only a sprain. His eyes appeared normal to look at. He agreed he would come up to the surgery for a proper examination.

'Let me give you a hand back to the house,' I offered,

and, hobbling painfully up the steps and across the garden, he leaned heavily on me till we finally reached the chair in the small front room.

'Would you take a wee dram with me?' he asked. 'The bottle's in the cupboard over there,' he continued, pointing to it. 'The glasses are underneath.' I fetched them.

The furnishings inside the house had not changed since Uncle Tom's day. Even the bed was still downstairs.

Clumsily he poured two measures of whisky, spilling some. He passed me one. We chatted socially for a few minutes.

'It's a beautiful place, this,' he said, after a while. 'When you've lived most of your life, like I have, in a tenement, where there's only one door, and every window looks out at somebody else's brick wall, you can appreciate it.' He waved his hand at the back door. 'Look out there, at that garden, at all that space,' and, swinging round in his chair, he pointed out of the open front door. 'Freedom,' he said, 'the freedom to come and go.' He rubbed his eyes. He was obviously not seeing very well. I assumed it was the whisky.

He passed me his glass. 'Pour me another one,' he requested. 'Only a small one, mind. I can't really afford this stuff now, you know.' He watched me pour one each.

'Thanks,' he said. 'If I'd let myself pour them, I'd have made them too big.'

I remembered the little girl's words, 'Drunk again'. 'Do you have a problem, then, drinking too much?' I asked casually.

He laughed. 'No more than any other true Scotsman. I enjoy a drink, too much on occasions, but the trouble is, I can't afford it while I'm still out of work.'

'You've not got a job yet, then?' I asked, equally casually.

'No,' he said candidly. 'But I've had more offers than I can cope with.'

I waited for him to continue.

119

'The trouble is,' he said at last, 'I can't do them. The holiday camp wanted a maintenance man for the swimming pool, but I don't understand plumbing. I could have had a job on the Council, cutting grass, but I don't understand the mechanics of mowers.' He looked at me earnestly. 'It wouldna be right to take on a job if you couldna do it, would it?'

I nodded some sort of agreement. 'What is your job? What can you do, then?'

'Och, anything,' he said casually. 'I've been a taxi driver for twelve years, a railway porter, had a stint on the boats, all sorts of things. To be honest, I'm enjoying the rest and doing a bit of gardening. I'm learning how to make my own wine, and grow my own tobacco.'

I rose to go, and thanked him for the whisky, glad that I had not had to sample his attempts at home-made wine. I assumed that if it tasted anything like the revolting smell of his home-grown tobacco, it would be undrinkable. If he had too much of it and fell down a hole in his own garden, I could do no more than help him out.

I returned to the task of mowing my own lawn.

The summer progressed to autumn. As I passed Mr McIntyre's cottage, in the course of daily routine, it seemed that nothing changed. The old lean-to greenhouse appeared as decrepit as ever, and a losing battle seemed to be progressing in the garden. Parts of it were hacked and harried to bare earth on occasion, and parts regrew waist-high with weeds. Gossip hinted that now he was brewing his own wine, Mr McIntyre was sinking into a state of gentle inebriation for most of the time, but I was not consulted.

*   *   *

The same small girl came racing up the drive just as I returned from evening surgery. This time her eyes were round with excitement, and she and her bicycle positively steamed with exertion.

'Mr McIntyre's fell down that hole again,' she gasped. 'I'll go and tell Dad.' Heaving her front wheel round, she turned and raced off.

I followed her out. He was indeed down his hole, and in quite a bad way. Shocked and dazed, he sat clutching the old boiler for support. His left ankle was obviously broken. There was no doubt that he would have to be admitted to hospital straight away.

I told him what I thought. He nodded in agreement. As we were talking, I became aware that his eyes were abnormal. He was staring at me with a fixed gaze, more reminiscent of blindness, and despite it being a lovely light late summer evening, his pupils were widely dilated. His hands, too, had a coarse tremor, as he poked his pipe at his mouth, and missed several times before he finally got it into position. He took several deep sucks at it, taking the foul smoke deep into the base of his lungs.

'Can you hop up the steps if I help you?' I asked him. 'Then I can take you straight into hospital, save waiting for the ambulance.'

While I held him upright, he tried. He had no sense of balance whatever, and the two of us swayed and heaved and slipped and fell for several minutes before I managed to return him to his original position.

The attempt to stand and climb out had given him a severe sense of sea sickness.

Seated back on his boiler again, looking grey and sweaty, he clung on to me.

'God, man,' he muttered, 'that was awful.' He retched again. 'What the hell's goin' on?'

His foul-smelling pipe had fallen to the floor, disappearing between the side of the boiler and a heap of moss-encrusted bricks. It was burning well, and from the crack emerged, at first a trickle, then a cloud of bonfire smoke. I kicked some loose rubble and soil over it – it was beginning to make me feel sick too – and stamped it well in.

'What the hell's goin' on?' he said again. 'Never been like this before.'

'Not that pipe making you ill?' I asked.

'Och, no,' he said, waving a feeble hand. 'That's just an old batch of tobacco that's got a wee bit dry.'

Sitting precariously on his boiler, he looked and felt even worse. 'When did all this come on?' I asked.

'Just now,' He said. 'I was fine till I fell down the hole, and it's got worse ever since.'

The small female member of the family, still clutching the handlebars of her equally small bike, appeared against the skyline, and looked curiously down.

'Daddy's coming,' she said. 'I told him you'd be down here.'

Within a very few minutes, several members of the family had appeared, and with collective ease had lifted out the prostrate Mr McIntyre and carried him to his cottage.

I phoned for the ambulance, and also spoke to the orthopaedic surgeon on duty. 'It's very strange,' I said. 'He's certainly got a broken ankle that needs pinning, but there's something else as well. I haven't had a chance to examine him properly, but I don't know if he's just a heavy drinker of his own home-made wine, or whether he could have some nervous disorder – multiple sclerosis, perhaps.'

Mr McIntyre was soon on his way to hospital, where they operated, and fixed his very badly broken ankle.

Next morning, routinely, I went to see him. He was still very dizzy, complained bitterly of nausea, headache, abdominal pain, and his ankle was extremely sore. Together, the surgeon and I examined him. The signs were virtually the same: loss of vision, fixed pupils, impaired sense of balance and loss of sensation in his hands and feet. It just did not add up to anything, alcoholic or otherwise, and we were both mystified.

'Still,' mused the surgeon, as we discussed it and arranged all the usual blood and urine tests, 'if it is multiple sclerosis, which seems the most likely, there is nothing that can be done at this stage.'

I agreed. Multiple sclerosis, or MS, as it is usually called, is an incurable disease of the nervous system, which progresses over the years inevitably to death, with remissions and relapses in a most unpredictable manner along the way. Only very rarely was the onset as abrupt as this.

I asked Mr McIntyre discreetly about his alcohol consumption, and if he had noticed any symptoms over the preceding months – loss of sensation, tingling, slurred speech and so on. He cheerfully admitted imbibing freely of his own home brew, and smoking his own home-cured tobacco, but vehemently denied excesses. He also admitted that the unsteadiness had been increasing over the past few months. It seemed almost inevitable that he was developing MS.

'What is this MS?' asked Mr McIntyre a few days later. We were still completely baffled. His blood tests were as confusing as his physical signs. His blood alcohol was virtually nil, he had a marked acidosis and a very high blood sugar, which should have meant he had diabetes; but he was not thirsty, had no sugar in his wee, and if anything was passing very little. Diabetics produce volumes. His liver function tests, too, were disturbed, but it was not the picture of a chronic alcoholic. These tests should all have been normal with MS, but the signs in his nervous system could only be explained by an MS-type illness: it seemed the only explanation. Mr McIntyre was as anxious for knowledge as we were. He wanted to know all about MS. His blood tests returned to normal in a very short space of time.

'It's a very variable disease,' I explained to him. 'Let's regard the brain as a computer. This receives all the information from the various sense organs, eyes, ears, joint position, muscle tone, etc. The computer collates this all together, and then sends signals to all the various motor organs, muscles and so on, telling them what to do. The nerves are just like telephone wires that transmit the information to and fro.'

'I see,' he nodded. Though still unable to see properly, and very dizzy if he moved, we could see, and he could sense, a marked improvement in his condition.

'Think as if the nerves were actual telephone wires,' I went on, 'with an inner conducting core and an outer insulating sheath, keeping the signals separate. The spinal cord is really just an enormous bundle of thousands of telephone wires, each one carrying a different message to and from the brain.'

'Ah, yes,' he said, nodding his head in agreement. 'That's why you can't feel your feet if you break your spine. I'd always wondered why that was. It's obvious when you think of it – the wires are disconnected.'

'Yes,' I said, 'but you can have the same effect if the wires are still intact, but short-circuited. If something takes away the insulation round the wires, they will all touch and short each other out, so very confused signals pass in all the wrong directions, and most don't get through at all.'

I paused, waiting until I was sure he had understood.

'In MS, the nerve channels are disconnected in bits and pieces along the whole spinal cord. It's as if someone had spattered acid all over the system, the acid dissolving the insulation where it landed, so that all the wires at that point short-circuit and don't work, or are affected so that they send out erroneous signals to the computer. The nerves not affected work normally.'

'I think I get it,' he said. 'How long does it take for the nerves to mend?'

'It's impossible to predict,' I told him honestly. 'Sometimes weeks, sometimes months, and sometimes never.'

'And you think I've got it?'

'Yes,' I said.

Mr McIntyre recovered in days. The speed of recovery cast doubts on the accuracy of the diagnosis. It had all come on too fast, and improved too quickly. The abnormal blood tests had settled down and returned to normal very quickly, too. The diagnosis of MS remained probable, but not proven, so that by the time several weeks had passed and his ankle bones had united sufficiently well for him to be allowed home to fend for himself, there was no detectable evidence of any disease of his nervous system.

He was discharged with orders to report to me after a couple of weeks. Within ten days he had sent for me. His symptoms had all recurred, but with less dramatic suddenness than before.

Seated this time in his own armchair, he told me how the impairment of sight and balance had crept up on him, of how his fingers tingled and burned, and of how he had lost the sensation in his feet. The nausea and headache were just beginning.

Without further ado, he was back in hospital. Examination and investigation produced exactly the same picture as before. Clinically he appeared to have MS, but again with acidosis, raised blood sugar, and liver damage. It just did not make sense.

Fred, our visiting consultant, stood at the end of the bed, and scratched his head.

'Never seen anything like it,' he said. 'Do all the tests again, and we'll see how he is next week.'

By the next week, as before, he had virtually fully recovered. We sent him home, assuming that he did have a virulent variation of MS. In response to his direct questioning, I warned him that his troubles would continue, and in all probability could become much worse.

After a few days, I called to see him.

'Who is it?' he called from his small back room. Shouting out my name, I marched in on him.

'I've just come to see how you are,' I said.

'Bide a wee moment,' he said, and, looking up at me, 'You'll no tell the law, will ye?'

Apart from being very guilty, he seemed to be in excellent health. I looked at what he was doing.

'Just wait for this to finish boiling,' he said, moving the flame of a gas camping stove higher under the old petrol tin hanging from the roof.

'I'm just brewing up some more whisky. Being all that while in hospital, I've no' had the time to brew any, and I'm right out.' He looked at me in a direct challenge. 'And if I have got that MS, and am going to lose ma power of movement, I may as well enjoy masel' as long as a can.'

Slowly, incredulously, I inspected his equipment. A five-gallon petrol tin hung from the old bacon hook in the roof on a piece of wire. It was swinging gently like a pendulum, while Mr McIntyre heated its bottom with the flames from his camping stove.

'What's in the can?' I asked.

'Fermenting grain and potatoes,' he replied. 'Seems better than grain alone.'

A ten-foot length of copper pipe, bent at one end and inserted into the spout of the petrol can, stretched across the room. The other end was stuck precariously under the handle of a bucket. Steam gushed out of both ends.

The whole stank like the distillery it so obviously was. We watched in silence as the vapour from the boiling fluid in the petrol tin cooled in the copper pipe, reverted to the fluid state, and dripped into the bucket.

Mr McIntyre gazed at it with pride. 'A wee bitty burnt sugar to colour it, and in a drop o' lemonade, ye can hardly tell the difference,' he boasted.

I watched in fascination as the process came to an end. It bothered me that there was only one bucket. In the dim recesses of my memory, I seemed to recall learning in school chemistry that the wood alcohol came off first and

126

had to be discarded, the next off was the drinkable bit, and the tail end contained all the bad-tasting poisons. This, too, should be thrown away.

I voiced my fears. 'Och, no,' he dismissed them. 'Not done me any harm so far.'

Wood alcohol was methyl alcohol, as in methylated spirits. It was a poison that produced blindness and nerve damage. Speechless, I watched him carefully bottle it. 'I've just got to press my tobacco,' he said. 'Then we can go into the other room.'

He walked over to the window, and lifted a half hundredweight weight off a plank of wood. Underneath was a mass of vegetation that looked like a compost heap.

'Tobacco?' I questioned.

'Surely,' he said.

I looked at him, and then at it. 'Are you sure?' I said.

He nodded confidently. 'Got the method from this book here.' He picked it up and passed it to me.

It was an old book, eighty years old, a sort of children's encyclopaedia that explained all the complicated technology of the era – how to make leather, beer, wine, cement, steel and so on. It was open at the page on how to distil spirits.

He took the book back, and flicked through the pages. 'Here,' he said. 'Tobacco.'

I looked. There was a brief description of how the leaves were picked, dried in the sun, and then packed, dampened with rum and molasses, and pressed flat with a large weight.

'I've done all that,' he said proudly. 'Look at this paragraph here: "The burning quality of the tobacco is enhanced if dampened with a little ethylene glycol."' His eyes lit up. 'Ethylene glycol's nuthin' but common old antifreeze. It does burn much smoother if I put some on.'

He reached under the shelf and produced a gallon tin of antifreeze. Liberally and lovingly, he sprinkled it over his tobacco, replaced the board, and heaved the weight back on the top.

I looked at him in amazement. 'How long have you been doing this?' I asked. 'Making your own spirits and putting antifreeze all over your tobacco?'

'Ever since I've been here,' he replied. 'As soon, in fact, as I'd grown the tobacco.'

'Just about as long as you've been ill,' I told him. 'I am very delighted to tell you,' I said, 'that you quite definitely have not got MS.'

He looked at me in some surprise.

'You, you silly man,' I told him, 'are suffering from a classic case of neuritis, secondary to poisoning. It's the wood alcohol in your brew, and the glycol in the tobacco. They're poisoning you. Whyever didn't I think of it before? For God's sake, throw it all away. Burn it. Just don't have any more.'

He continued looking at me, slowly realising that it was indeed so. Everything fitted.

I picked up his book and passed it back to him. 'You'd better burn this, too,' I said. 'Wherever did you get it?'

'It was one of Great-Grandfather's,' he replied. 'All his old books are upstairs. He left them all to me when he died, but Uncle Tom had the use of them during his lifetime.'

I stared at him in amazement. 'He was your Uncle Tom?'

'Great Uncle. I thought you knew.'

'But you're Scottish,' I said stupidly. 'From Glasgow.'

'Yes,' he said. 'But Uncle Tom and my grandfather were brothers.'

'Your grandfather was named Arthur,' I said.

'Aye, that's right.'

'Well, how come you originate from Scotland?'

'My grandmother was Scottish. She came down to Lowestoft for the herring. Lots of Scots girls used to come. They gutted the herring and put them in the barrels. She met Grandfather coming down on the train. He was shovelling coal at the station.'

128

'Sounds very romantic,' I said.

'Oh, it was. Great-Grandfather couldn't stand the smell of the fish, and her father refused to meet him because he wasn't Scottish.'

'What happened, then?'

'They went off together. He got a job as a coachman, in a nunnery of all places, and Grandmother got pregnant.'

'Were they married?'

'No. They were going to, only Grandfather caught typhoid. There was a hospital in the nunnery, and they all got it. Grandfather died, but Grandmother got better. The baby was my mother.'

'Ah,' I said. It was all coming together.

'They had strange morals in those days,' he continued. 'Her family disowned her as she'd got pregnant by an Englishman. His father wouldn't have anything to do with her, but every week until she died, the old man sent her Arthur's wages. That's all she had to live on. She never married, brought up my mother all on her own, in a tenement in Glasgow.'

He looked at me. 'It's a daft world,' he said. 'My mother had me illegitimately. The only money she had, Uncle Tom sent her. She never met him, and now she's dead I find that the old man had left her the house, but she couldn't have it till Tom died.'

I agreed: it is a daft world. 'Why did they put Arthur in the wall at Godley?'

'That's where he died. He was one of the first to be cremated. I think it was really his cremation that upset both families so. They put his ashes in an urn, and sealed it up in the memorial wall of St John's Church, at Godley.'

'Ah,' I said. The mystery was explained. I helped him throw out his spirits and tobacco onto the compost heap where they belonged.

'I suppose I'd better get a job,' he said.

'Yes,' I replied, as I walked away.

11

Slowly the realisation dawned: I was a proper farmer again. The veneer of medicine and civilisation, so painfully applied in my youth and adolescence, was now cracked and peeling. The agricultural peasant, within the city suit and the cultured bedside manner, was not only bursting to get out but had already relegated the stethoscope to the back pocket.

Growing a crop of strawberries was one thing, proper farming was another. I was riding on the top of a combine harvester again, but this time over my own field, and watching my own wheat come tumbling down the elevators. Satisfying as it did some primaeval inner urge within, it was not, unfortunately, going to accomplish my proper day's work, but it was an experience I savoured, a special moment.

It was only a small field of wheat, four acres that Sir Percy had originally planted with leeks. The crop had been a dismal failure, the land thick, heavy clay, and the workforce had declined to dig out all those miserable looking leeks with a fork, by hand.

They had still been in the ground when we had taken over the farm – thin, rotting and smelly.

I had sought advice on the best way of harvesting them. All the experts agreed that they were not worth the bother. 'Plough them in,' had been the universal advice.

As a great favour, William had done just that, and while he was at it had planted the ground with wheat, to put it to some use that season, while I and my aged workforce thought up better plans for it.

It was his combine that was now working my field. In my

city suit, and with my stethoscope still in my pocket, I exulted in the dust and the dirt and the noise, and held my hands out under the tail of the combine, from where the rejected straw is thrown out, mixed with the chaff which has been blown the length of the machine by enormous fans. I was feeling for any grain which, instead of falling through, had been blown over the riddles.

I waved for the driver to stop. 'Shut her down a bit, David,' I said. 'There's some coming over.'

He stared at me, the look of astonishment frozen on his face.

After the flashing knives at the front open mouth of the combine have cut the standing corn, the elevators carry it up to the threshing drum. This is a revolving cylinder of hammers smashing the straw across an open steel mesh. The straw passes on, but the corn and the chaff fall through. The wind from the fans blows the chaff to the back; the weight of the grains of wheat causes them to fall, down through the blast of air, onto the shaking riddles at the front. Elevators carry the corn up to the bin, and the last of the rubbish is carried off to join the straw, as it is thrown out of the back of the machine.

To obtain perfect separation of wheat and straw requires a little knowledge and some skill – how far to open up the drum, the fans and the air intakes. Each field is different. The relative dampness of the straw, and the size and weight of the wheat and the chaff, all dictate minor adjustments.

David stared at me as I brushed the dust off the sleeves of my suit. He couldn't have known that I had spent all my student summers contract-driving a combine. He only knew me as 'The Doc' and our only previous contact had been via his pregnant wife.

I remembered it had been a rather difficult forceps delivery in the tiny back room of a small row of terraced farmworkers' cottages. He had come with her afterwards for all

131

the routine baby clinic visits, to hold the baby. His wife had a terrible phobia about needles.

'Close her down about two notches each side?' I suggested.

He nodded agreement and, taking a spanner out of his pocket, knelt on the ground each side of the combine to make the adjustments.

'I'll take her,' I said, 'and you check the corn, see if that's enough.'

I climbed up into the cab of the great, lumbering machine and, working the controls automatically, surprised myself at the easy execution of skills that I had thought were long forgotten. In a sort of day dream, I went all the way round the field, with David checking the straw and adjusting the fan air inlet as we travelled.

'I didn't know you could drive a combine, sir,' he said respectfully, as I climbed back down the steps. He had never called me 'sir' before, not even when I had delivered his son. I felt very flattered.

Reluctantly leaving the past behind, I walked away, back to the present. The cut stubble scratched against my shoes, and the newly exposed bare earth was surprisingly moist, sheltered as it had been by the dense wheat from the heat of the summer sun. It would only remain so for a few short hours, before it dried and baked to the hardness of concrete. The tyre tracks of the combine cut cleanly and crisply into the soil, leaving deep-patterned lines across the field. The only too familiar smell of corn dust and diesel oil kept dragging me back to my childhood.

But this time it was not someone else's wheat in someone else's field, it was my own wheat in my own field, something which I had never thought I could ever see; something that was not compatible with the art of medicine. It affected me very profoundly. I walked to the car. The afternoon visits and the evening surgery had still to be done.

* * * *

Mrs Willoughby was not in the least agricultural. Her refined suburban elegance made me acutely conscious of the smell of corn dust about my person. I was aware too, that my hands, although socially clean, were not clean enough for me to lay them on any part of her exposed skin.

'Excuse me,' I said, as she reclined back onto her embroidered sheets and awaited the examination. 'May I just use your bathroom?'

She was not the sort of person I could tell about my bubbling pride in this, my own very first harvest. My news and experiences were irrelevant in this house, but there were many other houses where, though I could do little good in the way of cure, such exchange of information made both doctor and patient feel much happier, and lessened the burden of illness.

Mrs Willoughby expected, and usually got, a cure. I had been summoned for one purpose, and one purpose only, and that was to clear her chest of a very mild bronchitis. Somehow she always managed to get an attack before each of her big social occasions. Really, it was more of a nervous bronchospasm, an attack of asthma, but since a few days in bed on antibiotics always cleared it magically, there was little point in arguing with her diagnosis.

She had been one of my very first patients, and indubitably would still be there at the last. Childless, and although actually divorced from her husband, she liked it to be generally assumed that she was a young widow. Ever since our first meeting, I had been very conscious that she had only one topic of conversation, and that was herself. Her sole interest was self-adornment. If she couldn't wear it, flash it, or drape it decorously about her person, she wasn't interested.

On one previous occasion, when she had been genuinely

ill, I had seen her without her make-up. I had noticed surprising traces of grey roots showing through her normally exquisite dark hair, but I was quite sure no one else had ever been allowed to witness such a thing, especially her late husband.

Her breasts fascinated me. At some stage in her youth, she had had them surgically enlarged. Several plastic bags full of some oily silicone fluid had been inserted between the breast tissue and the chest wall. As the years had passed, the bags had become infected, and had moved, so that they became visible under the skin. Both breasts had become such tangled knots of very painful lumpy scar tissue and plastic bags full of oil, that further surgery was required to remove the silicone. The operation had not been a success. Cosmetically, the last result was worse than the first. Crammed into a supporting bra, enough soft skin on each side bubbled up to give the appearance of enticing normality, but without the bra they hung miserably down, deformed, painful, and scarred. I was always amazed at how little this appeared to worry her, but it seemed that so long as the outward appearance was maintained, the inner reality was not important. Naturally, it seemed, no man ever touched them. They were for show only, artificial icing on a cake in a shop window.

She had been warned many years previously that there was now a high probability of the development of potentially malignant lumps in such maltreated tissue, so that each time she developed bronchitis, the lumps were checked for visible and palpable change.

I returned from the bathroom, hands medically clean, and smelling of her perfumed soap, but very aware of the residual hint of corn dust and diesel oil. Mrs Willoughby gave no sign of having noticed anything amiss, but I was acutely conscious of the enormous gulf between the two parts of my life – the medical career and the agricultural instincts.

Mrs Willoughby lay back in her bed, awaiting the examination, those awfully deformed breasts fully exposed. Carefully I applied my stethoscope to her chest. It sounded very normal.

'There's nothing wrong with my chest,' she said. 'That was just an excuse to get you to call and see me at home.'

I looked up at her. She smiled. For the first time in my presence, her facial make-up moved, out of that fixed photographic model's pose, into a human expression.

She looked down at her breasts. 'Will I be able to feed a baby?' she asked casually. 'Not that it really matters at my age. The books say that very few first-time mothers over forty do.'

She saw the expression on my face. 'That's why I've asked you to come. You see, I'd like you to confirm that I'm really pregnant.'

Very carefully I assessed her physically. She offered no information about how and why she could have become pregnant, and I did not ask.

There definitely was a hint of deeper pigmentation around the nipples of those poor distorted breasts; through the vaginal speculum the cervix definitely showed that characteristic translucent blue colour. Internally, her womb was positively enlarged to about the size of a twelve-week pregnancy.

'Yes, you are,' I said, as I finished and repaired back to her bathroom to wash my hands again. The smell of cornfield and machinery was very much less noticeable.

I came back into her bedroom. She had dressed again, and was bubbling with emotion, wanting instant answers to all her questions. Mothers expecting their first babies at forty-one need a lot of careful handling. I tried to answer most of them, and persuaded her to come and see me for the full antenatal routine. The subject of male involvement in her condition did not arise.

I realised, as I left the house, that despite her apparent

135

total self-interest and self-reliance, she was in fact very alone, and very vulnerable. As a patient she would need a great deal of moral support from me. I realised, too, that despite owning a field of wheat, I really was, after all, a doctor at heart.

12

I didn't learn the story all at once: there was far too much to tell. It came out in small, individual, disjointed sentences, like the pieces of a jigsaw puzzle, the picture building erratically, a bit at a time. For a long time, the developing picture made no sense, but as the remaining pieces came together, I could appreciate the whole, while remaining aware that there was much I still did not know.

The day I had the first inkling was a day like any other, in the middle of a normal, mundane surgery; a day of people with coughs, colds, aches and pains, and mostly needing certificates.

She was a young girl of twenty-two, who looked much more like thirty-two, a patient of Mac's, whom I had not met before.

Mac was on holiday. It was our quiet season, mid-November, when all the holidaymakers had gone home and the winter rush had not yet begun. Mac always went off for two weeks' golf in Scotland in November. I was doing his work as well as my own.

Her name was Margaret Chillingford, and she sat subdued and submissive in the chair by my desk. She looked as if she had always been subdued and submissive, and she told me she did not feel well.

No more, no less: she just didn't feel well. I asked her in what way. She shrugged her shoulders dejectedly. The shrug said that it was of no importance, no matter. Her feelings had never been of any consequence, and never would be. Explanations were difficult, meaningless. She just didn't feel well, a non-specific sense of malaise and depression. An aura of sadness and helplessness emanated from her, a pathetic resignation to her fate.

137

I studied her more carefully in the chair. She did not return my look, merely stared at the floor. She was not going to be one of those quick, easy consultations, in and out in five minutes with a prescription and a certificate.

This was a presentation that could cover anything from flu to tuberculosis, from anaemia to unwanted pregnancy, from the boyfriend in prison to a developing cancer. She was not particularly communicative.

Her whole attitude gave out passive acceptance, inevitable acceptance of whatever was in store. I was the doctor: whatever I said would be right; she would do as she was told. What she felt about it was irrelevant. It was just that she was unwell, unable to cope, and seeking relief. The way she sat miserably slumped in the chair said that she did not expect any.

'Tell me about it,' I said.

She shrugged her shoulders again.

'Nothing to tell,' she said.

The medical history would have to be dragged out of her, word by word, system by system, function by function, one fact at a time.

I started with the digestive system: how was she eating, discomfort after meals, bowels regular, losing weight?

The answers to all my questions were uninterested negatives. The only information I gained was that she could not be bothered to cook, and were it not for her four-year-old son, would not do so.

I changed to the respiratory system. No cough, no shortness of breath, no chest pains, no nothing.

Routinely I went through the catalogue of bodily functions, getting only more uninterested negatives.

No, she was not pregnant, her periods were normal. She was not on the pill. By exclusion, her problem must therefore be one of emotion, a reactive depression to circumstances.

I enquired about her circumstances. The same negative

lack of interest. She lived alone, apart from her son, in a small council house. She had no job, social security paid the rent, and sent her a fortnightly cheque. It was enough for their needs.

No, she said, no problems with parents, hadn't seen them for years, didn't want to see them. Didn't even know where they were.

No, she'd never been married. No she hadn't a steady relationship, no boyfriend. Nothing since the birth of her son.

'What about before he was born?' I asked. 'You must have had a steady relationship then.'

Again the shrug of the shoulders.

'Not really.'

'The baby's father. You must have had some sort of relationship with him.'

The tips of her shoulders moved, negatively.

'How did you conceive the baby?' I asked.

The shoulders moved. 'The usual way.'

'Didn't you have any affection for him?'

'Not really.'

'Why did you let him make love to you, then?'

For the first time she looked at me. 'Couldn't say "No", I suppose,' she said. 'Never have been able to.'

There was a long silence.

'What about since the baby?' I asked.

'No,' she said. 'Nothing. I haven't. I don't go out any more.'

'Are you lonely, all by yourself all day and all night?'

'Suppose so,' she said. 'Haven't really thought about it. My boy's with me. He's company.'

'He'll be going to school soon,' I said.

'I know,' she replied. There was just that little edge of concern in her voice, a marked change from the negative uninterest. 'It'll be better when he does.'

I waited for her to continue, but she didn't.

'Is he spending too much time alone, as well as you, then?' I asked gently.

'No,' she said. 'That's not the problem. He's no problem. It's me, I'm frightened what I'm going to do to him.'

I waited. It seemed like a very long wait.

'Tell me,' I said quietly.

She looked up at me; her hands came together, and the fingers twisted and writhed. Anguish was written all over her face. Two tears came into the corner of each eye.

'I'm going to be like my stepfather,' she said, 'and I don't want to be. I can't stand it.'

The tears flowed freely. I nodded, waiting again for her to continue. She wiped her eyes with the back of her hand.

'My boy, when he's in the bath, I can't keep my eyes off him, off his little privates,' she said. 'When he was little, in nappies, I used to wash him, and apart from the fact that he was a little boy, think nothing of it. Now, I'm so terrified of fondling him, of what I might do to him, I have to shut my eyes, and wash him quick.'

The confession had exhausted her. She trembled slightly, mute, tearstained, remorseful, waiting to be punished.

'How long have you felt like this?' I asked.

'Oh, always,' she said. I watched the helpless shrug of the shoulders again. 'He's four now. It's been bad for the past two years. I've never dared tell anybody before. I've been so ashamed, I haven't dared to go out. I didn't mean to tell you today.'

'Your stepfather,' I said gently. 'Tell me about him.'

'Nothing to tell, really,' she said. 'I was illegitimate. Mother had a lot of boyfriends. There was a lot of them came and went, then we moved here.'

'To the house you live in now?'

'That's right. Mother was the tenant. When she ran away, they let me have it. Stepfather hung around longer than any of the others. He moved in permanently, and they got married when I was eight.'

'How did you get on with him?'

'All right. He used to play with me, and give me sweets. He used to let me get into bed with him, and fondle me, you know, all over. He liked me to play with him. It was exciting making him get an erection.'

She paused again, her hands resting in her lap, her eyes looking at the floor, but far away. She seemed somehow relaxed, but still pale and taut, as the memories came pouring out.

'I remember the first time he entered me. I was nine. We'd tried several times before – it was a bit of a game. I enjoyed it – but that time it hurt. He was so strong, he used so much force, and wouldn't stop when I cried.

'He gave me a big packet of sweets, and said I was his special girl. The next time it hardly hurt at all, and after that not at all.'

'Did you enjoy it?' I asked, after a while.

'I enjoyed the sweets, I enjoyed being special. It was our secret.'

'Did your mother know?'

'Must have done, but she never said anything.'

'How long did this go on?'

'All the time. It wasn't till I grew up that I realised it was wrong. I suddenly realised that boys at school could be fun, and then he started beating me. He made me feel guilty and ashamed just talking to boys.'

'How old were you then?'

'About fourteen. He'd really beaten me one night because I'd said "No, I wasn't in the mood". He beat me so much, that he only had to look at me and jerk his head, and I'd have to go upstairs, lie naked on the bed, and wait for him to come up.

'That came to be the routine. I'd come home from school, he was unemployed, home all day; he would look up the stairs, jerk his head, and I'd go to my bedroom. If he knew I wanted to go out, he'd make me wait naked and cold, till nightfall, so I couldn't go.'

I made a mental note to look up her stepfather's notes, see what sort of a man he was, find out if I knew him. Somewhere in the back of my memory was something I just couldn't recall, but I had a feeling I knew him. The address and the chronic unemployment were familiar, but neither Mac nor I had ever remotely suspected anything like this.

She resumed her story. It seemed that in telling it, she was easing herself of a great burden.

'That was when I went to the police,' she said. 'I told them all about it, about him, and about being beaten, and having to wait naked for him for hours. I spoke to a policeman first. He was very embarrassed, so I had to tell it all over again to a woman, and I could see she didn't believe me. I had to wait for hours for them to go home and speak to my mother, and him, and when they came back, they told me it was all a pack of lies, my teenage imaginings, and if I signed a piece of paper saying I'd made it all up, they'd let me go home. If I didn't, they'd charge me, and send me to prison.

'What did you do?'

'I signed their bit of paper, But I just couldn't go home. I ran away.'

'And you've never told anyone about this before?'

'No point. They wouldn't listen, wouldn't believe me. They'd only despise me if they knew. A common prostitute since the age of nine.'

'I've got no reason to disbelieve you,' I said. 'You're not the first child to be abused, nor unfortunately, the last.'

I could also believe that she had never told anyone else before. Had I not probed and searched, she would not have told me. Now that she had finally shared her awful guilty secret, the first steps could be taken on the road back to normality, and the lifting of that self-denigrating depression.

I reassured her that her emotions towards her son, her own lack of desire for other human companionship, were

142

all a part of the childhood wound, and now that we had opened it, allowing all the festering poisons to emerge, it was a situation that would correct itself. The old adage about time being the great healer was also very true.

She seemed eager to hang on my words, yet to disbelieve me at the same time. I had established contact with her. She would leave a large part of her guilt behind her, when she walked out of the surgery. It was the start of her first healing relationship.

'Dr Mac will be back next week,' I said. 'Now that we've brought it all out into the open, I think you will begin to feel better. We ought to keep an eye on you. I'll leave a note for him, and he can check on your progress.'

'Please, no,' she said. 'Don't tell Dr Mac. I'd be too ashamed if he ever found out. Can I come and see you instead?'

'Of course,' I told her, 'but you were the victim. You have been made to feel guilty and ashamed for what was done to you. It isn't until we can clear all this shame and guilt out of the way that you can begin to recover. Dr Mac will understand, he will help enormously, probably more than I can.'

We agreed that I should tell him, but that she would come to see me instead. Mac would not be exactly pleased that I had taken over one of his patients, but he would not argue. I knew he would understand.

When Mac came back from his fortnight's golfing holiday, I returned all his patients I had seen to his care. We discussed them all. I explained to him about Margaret Chillingford's confession, and how I had accidentally stumbled on it.

'Makes sense,' he said at last. 'There was always something odd about that family. Nothing you could put your finger on. She was a bit furtive, running about like a frightened rabbit. He was just ordinary, nothing special. In and out of work, like so many of them, but they always seemed to avoid me, hurried away when I passed. Never really took any notice of them.'

143

'What about the daughter, Margaret? Anything odd about her?'

'Not really,' he said, thinking. 'They weren't a family who troubled me a lot. She got into trouble with the police, was put into care and finished up in a remand centre, but then so did a lot of others.'

He puffed at his pipe for a few moments.

'Come to think of it, when she came back she was already pregnant, and her parents moved out. It was said that they'd emigrated to Australia, but somehow I don't think they went, they just moved away. Because she was pregnant, the Council let her have the house.'

'Do you think she's telling the truth?' I asked.

'Difficult to say,' he replied, as he got his pipe going again. 'Like you, I've no reason to disbelieve her.'

Margaret Chillingford did come to see me again, once more in the middle of a routine surgery.

'Come in, sit down,' I said to her, as she hesitantly entered the room. She was still mousy, meek and submissive, but the aura of dejection and depression was not nearly so marked.

Once more, she sat and looked at the floor, and waited for me to speak.

'How are you?' I said, conversationally.

'Better, thanks.' She seemed more embarrassed and uncertain than non-communicative.

'How do you feel?'

'All right.'

There was a long wait. I could feel her uncertainty, her hesitancy to start a conversation, though the fact that she had come at all meant that she wanted to talk.

'What's on your mind?' I said.

She shrugged her shoulders in that familiar gesture. 'Everything and nothing.'

'Tell me about it, then.'

'Have you told Dr Mac?'

'Yes.'

'What did he say?'

'What I expected him to say. He said that it explained a lot, made things that had puzzled him clearer.'

'Nothing else?'

'We talked a lot about the guilt of being a victim, the inner shame of it, whereas in reality, if people knew, they would have sympathy and offer help, not condemnation.'

'He didn't mention Mother?'

'Only in the sense that she was as big a victim as you, could no more help what was going on than you could.'

There was a pause while she digested what I had said.

'He didn't say it was my fault they went away?'

'No. Should he have done?'

'No, no,' she said too quickly, and then went silent. I did not press the point.

She then changed the subject to her little boy, how she was thinking of finding a playschool for him, and how quickly he was growing up.

'You are much better,' I said. There was a long silence. It seemed that the conversation was over for today.

'Yes,' she said as she stood up. 'I am.'

'You'll come and see me next week?'

As she walked out, there was definitely an improvement in her carriage. Some of her depression had lifted.

I reported the conversation to Mac when we next met.

'I got the impression,' I told him, 'that she felt herself responsible for her parents moving out, almost that she drove them out.'

'Blackmail, you mean . . . ?'

'I don't know. I don't think so, but . . . '

And that was how we left it, the unanswered question hanging in the air.

It was several weeks before she came back again, in the mad, last-minute pre-Christmas rush. She had brought me a small present, a hairbrush. She sort of thrust it at me, wordlessly, expectantly.

145

I thanked her as I unwrapped it.

'It'll stop your hair falling all over your face,' she said.

I grinned at her. For the first time she smiled back. It gave her face a sort of elfin quality. Meek, submissive, just the same, but encouraging, too. The hint of a sexual invitation.

I was only too aware that she had seen the unconscious response on my face, that I had received her signal. Quickly, I brushed it away.

'How are you?' I asked.

'Better, thank you.'

We each waited for the other to speak, a vague feeling, of embarrassment almost, in the air. There was no doubt that she had made considerable strides on her road to recovery. She was no longer looking inward at her guilty emotions, but outward, far enough even to buy me a present and form a relationship.

We talked of the need for her to continue this process, of her vague and unsuccessful efforts to find a suitable play-school, and all around several other subjects. She did not mention her parents, nor the original preoccupation with her son's anatomy. I presumed that she was no longer obsessed with them.

Gently, wistfully, she wished me a happy Christmas, and slipped out through the door.

Mac always had New Year off. His house was open all day. Naturally, in passing, I stopped for a small glass of Scottish cheer.

He asked me about Margaret Chillingford and I told him about the hairbrush, and her silent hint, and my awkward response.

He laughed, and only half-joking said, 'You know, all little girls are women at heart. If she did something like that to her stepfather, she could have provoked him into something unstoppable. It does happen, you know. It's often a weak, rather than an evil man who does these things, and once done it's so much easier to do it the next time.'

That was something I had not thought about. Mac had seen all sides of life. He was a sceptic, a Scot, now well under the influence of his own Hogmanay hospitality, who had no illusions on the strengths and weaknesses of humanity. He had seen it all before, including streetwise nine-year-old Lolitas.

I joined him in another glass.

It was February before Margaret Chillingford came to the surgery again. The flu epidemic was in full spate. At least, we called it flu. It was probably only one of the many respiratory viruses doing the rounds, but it was prostrating the best of people.

It seemed the sort of virus that favoured those who admitted defeat early, those who retired to bed at the first sign and summoned their medical advisers for aspirin and sympathy. They recovered pretty smartly. The people who could not afford to be ill, for whatever reason, were the ones who struggled on for several days and then collapsed completely. Some of these were quite severely ill, with pneumonia and bronchitis, others apparently just totally exhausted. It seemed to take so many so long to recover.

Into the middle of this reappeared Margaret Chillingford. The flu virus had not visited her house – she said she felt very well. Her little son was doing fine, he'd started going to a playschool and loved it.

She had the elfin look – wistful, yet sad and longing. Her clothes were that little bit smarter, she did not look quite so much older than her age. The invitation on her face was still there.

I pushed the conversation to the other mothers she was meeting at the playschool. She was beginning to form relationships with them, her improvement was continuing, the depression was only intermittent.

'Are you going out in the evenings at all yet?' I asked, as part of the general enquiry.

'No,' she said slowly, the look in her eyes telling me, only too clearly, that if I cared to call, she'd be in.

Hastily, I changed the subject.

'Your mother,' I said. 'When we talked about her last, you said that she ran away. Are you ready to talk about her again yet?'

The aspect of sadness and apathy that had been so prominent on her first visit passed across her face. It stayed there for several moments.

'I'm sorry,' I carried on. 'If you don't want to talk about it . . .' realising that I had brought all her pain and guilt crashing back.

'No,' she said. 'I want to talk about it, but don't know where to start.'

I waited, aware that this would take time, time I hadn't got. There was a waiting room full of people outside.

'My mother,' she said. There was a long pause. 'Mother knew, and was ashamed.' Another pause. 'She ran away.' She began to speak in short sentences, with long pauses between them. The elfin sexual invitation on her face had gone. I realised how precarious was her recovery, how little she had really emerged from her past, and how vulnerable she still was.

'She ran away because I made her. At the police station she was scared, scared out of her wits. I could see she was. He was, too.

'After I ran away, the police brought me back. They were white-faced and shaking when they opened the door to the policeman. I used to run away, just to see their faces when the police brought me back.

'I never said a word. I couldn't tell anybody, especially after they said I'd made it all up, but they never knew. Each time they expected it.'

There was a longer pause, it must have lasted almost half a minute.

'They put me into care – that was awful – then I finished up in the remand centre.'

She looked up at me. 'When they let me out of there I was

148

seventeen, went down to London, and got pregnant. The police picked me up, and telephoned to say they were bringing me home. There was no one in, they'd gone, emigrated. Couldn't face me. I've been there alone ever since, me and the boy.'

'And you've never talked about it to anyone?'

'No. Who'd be interested? You're the only one who ever wanted to know.'

'Do you feel better for talking about it?'

'Don't know. Hadn't really thought about it till you asked. Perhaps I will tomorrow,' and she gave me the faintest elfin smile.

I showed her to the door. 'Keep in touch,' I said.

The flu epidemic seemed to last most of the spring. The daffodils were in full bloom when she came again. Mysterious would be a good word to describe her. Elfin, sad, haunting. Submissive, but not dejected. Very, very female.

She gave me that special smile.

'Sit down,' I offered, as she crossed the room to the chair. There was a certain grace in the way she walked, that had been missing before.

I smiled back at her. 'Are you as well as you look?'

'Yes, thank you. I am.'

'Tell me more,' I said.

'Nothing to tell. You said keep in touch. Here I am.'

Once more I was aware of her subtle, powerful invitation. She had dressed, and done her hair and make-up, very carefully. It was not the appearance of someone depressed and withdrawn, but of someone out to impress.

I was impressed. She was aware of the effect she was having on me. She smiled again, thoroughly enjoying it. She crossed her legs seductively.

'What nasty questions are you going to ask me today?' she said.

'Which ones would you like?' I replied. 'What other skeletons have you got in your cupboard that I ought to know about, and remove?'

She shook her head and laughed. 'None, and I feel so much better for the removal.' The laughter left her eyes for a moment, and was replaced by that haunting, longing look, the most overtly sexual invitation I had ever received. 'But you're welcome to try. I've been trying so hard not to come and see you, but I had to.'

I smiled at her, and put my hand on top of hers. 'Margaret,' I said gently, 'in my job, I have to see inside the hearts of many women. Many of those hearts could be mine for the taking. If I took one, I should have to take them all. Thank you for the offer.'

I picked up her hand, and held it. 'When someone has been emotionally where you have been, right to the very bottom of rock bottom, the hand that helps you up is always special.'

She nodded, those eyes so wistful, sad and appealing.

'You've given your heart not to me as a person, but to me as a doctor.'

'No.' She shook her head, but I interrupted.

'What it means is that you have recovered. You are now ready for that special person, that white knight in shining armour, ready for him to gallop in and carry you off into the sunset.'

She smiled again. 'White knights are not for me. If he came in wearing an old rusty tin can, with a bent lance, and riding on a donkey, if he looked like you, I'd take him.'

I grinned, the crisis was over. The fact that she had fallen for me was not to be unexpected, and I had managed to divert her emotions without damaging them again.

'I think it's time I got a job,' she said.

'What can you do?' I asked. 'Just in case I can help.'

'Secretarial,' she said. 'They taught me book-keeping and typing in that remand centre. I was quite good. I'm rusty, but it will soon come back. I'm available Monday, Wednesday and Friday mornings, when young Tony is at playschool.'

She rose to go, and walked to the door.

'Keep in touch,' I said. She half-turned, and gave me that wonderful, wistful, inviting smile again.

'I shall,' she said, and walked out through the door.

*　　　*　　　*

Brian Blotchell was a builder. He employed three men, and always had more work in hand than he could cope with. His wife was the brains of the business: she did all the paperwork, worked out the estimates, and sent in all the bills. He did the hard graft. His skills were recognised, and his prices deemed reasonable.

His world fell round his ears when his wife became pregnant. They already had three children, the youngest nineteen. Mrs Blotchell thought she was merely on the change, and getting fat.

She presented in the surgery complaining of swollen feet and headaches. She was six months gone, and had severe toxaemia of pregnancy. I admitted her to hospital there and then. She would have to spend the next three months there, having total bedrest.

Brian Blotchell was distraught. Without his wife to send out the bills and the estimates, his business would collapse. He told me he needed a part-time secretary to do his typing, and asked if I knew of one.

'I do know of one,' I said. 'Her name is Margaret Chillingford. She tells me she used to be good, but hasn't worked since the birth of her son four years ago. She says she's a bit rusty, but available on Monday, Wednesday and Friday mornings, while her boy is at playschool.'

She got the job. Brian found her services adequate. Not as good as his wife, he freely admitted, but at least she got the estimates typed out and the bills sent out on time. When his wife came out of hospital, with a brand-new baby daughter, Margaret was kept on, three half-days a week. It was an arrangement that suited them all.

151

One of the estimates she sent out was for a fairly large repair to a big block of flats, a job bigger, really, than Brian and his three men could cope with. They were awarded the contract.

Brian appeared in the surgery soon after the birth of his daughter, having hit his thumb with a seven-pound hammer. I removed the smashed nail and bandaged it up.

'How's work going?' I asked.

'Terrible,' he replied. 'I need three extra men. They say there's all this unemployment about, yet I can't even get a man to stand with his foot on the bottom of a ladder.'

'I think I know somebody,' I said.

13

Toby Willis's medical records went back a long way. They went back to even before he was born, to his father.

His father had chronic tuberculosis, a thin, wasted man, tiredly clinging to life, unable to work, and who had very few pleasures. He did not say a lot.

His mother was a large, angry woman. Angry that life had cheated her of so much; angry that she had finished up with a tuberculous invalid who earned no money; angry that she had to work, and that the only job she could get was to scrub out a factory at night; angry that she had become fat and unattractive; angry that no other man wanted her; angry that her only child was like his father – thin, quiet, wasted and tuberculous.

She was mean of spirit, and she had a lot to say.

Toby's father had just slipped away long before my time. I only knew him from what he had left behind – the tuberculosis he had given his son, and the bitterness he had left in the heart of his wife.

They lived in a small terraced Council house, not the cleanest or neatest in the row, but certainly the noisiest.

The noise came from the permanent state of war that existed between Toby's mother and her sister. The sister was equally bitter about her lot, and about her station in life. A spinster by choice, she could not stand men, and constantly berated the memory of her late brother-in-law, as a typical example of her low opinion of the opposite sex.

By the financial necessity of both parties, she had been taken in as a lodger soon after the disastrous marriage had taken place, and had remained ever since, quarrelling, shouting, and generally bemoaning her fate. She, too, had a job as an evening factory cleaner, which she hated.

153

Over the years, so many near neighbours on either side had complained to the housing department of the local Council, that they had, in desperation, specially selected for the adjoining houses elderly, very deaf tenants, who turned up the volume of their television sets and disregarded the noise.

In the midst of this, young Toby grew up, and watched his father die, quietly, unloved and unmourned.

Soon after this, his own tuberculosis had been discovered, and he had been taken away to hospital.

His medical records told the whole story – of a sad, solitary little boy, with tuberculous lesions in both lungs that just refused to heal, despite all the medication.

He had spent most of his childhood in and out of hospital, continually taking medicines, regularly subjected to various medical procedures, and finally, in his late teens, undergoing operations to remove the infected part of each lung.

On each side of his back were two huge scars, running roughly parallel with the outline of his shoulder blades, where the surgeons had gained access to his chest. The operations, and his general demeanour, had left him with a hunched, downcast appearance.

His mother and aunt had not been unkind to him; if anything they had overprotected him, keeping him away from other children, shut in the house, a silent witness to all their unhappy bickering, and with only deaf old neighbours with loud television sets for company, when they were both out working of an evening.

I had known him a long time. He had been one of the first patients to see me, coming for repeat medication and certificates. He had never worked in his life. As he grew from boyhood into adolescence, when most children think about earning a living, and of how they are going to spend the rest of their lives, both he and his two female guardians merely assumed that he would be just like his father, spending all his time at home, drawing sickness benefit.

154

It was inevitable that, sooner or later, having spent most of his days passing the time watching television, and his evenings drifting round the pubs, he should get into the drug scene. He regarded the escape from reality, given to him by the alcohol, the cannabis and the LSD, as the high points of his life. Without the kick that the drugs gave him there was no point to living.

Naturally, he did not have the money to pay for the drugs. Naturally, he went out and stole it, at first from his mother and aunt, then from his deaf neighbours, and finally from wider afield.

Naturally, being an ignorant, bumbling amateur at the game, he was soon caught by the police.

Naturally, when up before the magistrates for the third time in as many months, he was sent away for a spell of corrective training in one of Her Majesty's Borstal institutions.

He had returned from this a changed character. Tattooed on his fingers were the obligatory recognition signals of one ex-Borstal inmate to another – LOVE on the fingers of the left hand, and HATE on the fingers of the right.

His sense of the injustice of life was acute. The bitterness of his mother had passed largely over his head, it was just a part of the background noise, but now he was acutely aware that he was physically a nothing, socially a nothing, and, gazing into a future that he did not like, could see nothing to alter his prospects.

The good things of life that had not been provided for him, must, he had decided, be taken by force, stolen from those who had them.

At first, after his return from Borstal, he had gone back home, but the noise, the recriminations, the reiteration of old quarrels, had been too much, and he had moved out into a squalid bedsit.

Although he no longer needed regular medication and had been pronounced cured, apart from a routine yearly

155

X-ray, by the chest physicians, I was kept well informed of his progress by his mother.

Life had not been kind to her. Now, middle-aged, more than somewhat obese, rude and demanding, she sat once more in my surgery chair. Over the years I had grown used to her coarse manners, her bitterness, and her biased views of life.

I had discovered very early on that the soft answer turneth away wrath, and a sympathetic ear learned a great deal of relevant information. I had the feeling that, despite it all, she actually liked me. Her problems were insoluble.

'He's a ponce, a bloody ponce,' she shouted at me, in a voice loud enough to ensure that a full waiting room heard every word.

'Shh,' I said, nodding in the direction of the waiting room. 'They'll hear you out there. You mean Toby?'

'Of course I bloody well mean Toby. Who else?' she shouted back, her voice not one decibel lower.

'What's he done now?' I asked.

'He's gone to bloody London, that's what he's done, and put his arse-hole out for hire.'

'Shh. Not so loud,' I said again. 'There's no need to tell everyone out there.' I had visions of the shocked faces as they all sat up, jolted out of their waiting room silence; of how one or two would catch each other's eye and begin to giggle.

'He's a queer, a bloody queer,' she shouted again, glaring at me, 'with an arse-hole for sale.'

'Tell me about it,' I said, deliberately softly, hoping that if I lowered my voice, she would lower hers. It worked partially.

'He's gone to bloody London,' she said. Her outburst had calmed her. I waited for her to continue the story.

'He's in bloody prison again. They caught him trying to sell his arse-hole, the dirty little bugger.'

I looked at her sitting in the chair, unsure whether her

156

angry reaction was merely disgust that her son could do such a thing, or whether she was hiding her concern for him behind the coarse language.

The former, I felt. There was no deep philosophy behind her façade. She said what she thought, there were no deep feelings. She sat in the chair, a woman of sixteen stone, shaped like the proverbial sack of potatoes. Her powerful legs rested squarely on the floor, her uncleaned shoes, scrubbed at the toes, pointing unexpectedly inwards. Her hair had been permed and bleached so many times that it was now just a mass of scruffy tufts projecting at random from her skull, cut anyhow. Her eyes, blue and short-sighted, peered in indignation at me through thick, smeared lenses.

'When did he go?' I asked.

Still loud, but with some of the indignation muted, she said, 'Last week. He's in prison on a charge of male prostitution. I got this this morning.'

She dug in the commodious shopping bag on her knee, and produced a letter. She passed it over to me. It was from a solicitor, saying that he was acting for her son, Toby, under the legal aid scheme. Bail had been set on the surety of two thousand pounds, and if she cared to produce the necessary sum, Toby would be released into her care, pending the trial.

'Can you raise two thousand pounds?' I asked her. It seemed a ridiculous question.

'Not bloody likely,' she snapped back. 'And if he's inside for poncing, he can damn well stay there.'

She stared at me, steely-eyed through those pebble lenses.

'How can I help?' I asked. 'What can I do?'

'When he comes out, I want him done.' Those eyes glared at me. 'Get him castrated, stop that bloody nonsense. I'm not having any of that.'

It took quite a while for me to appreciate just what she was demanding. She took my silence for agreement.

'Well?' she said.

'We'll have to see what Toby thinks about it, when he comes home,' I eventually muttered, thinking that if he had any sense, Toby wouldn't come home.

'Good,' she snapped, and, gathering up her letter and stuffing it forcefully into her bag, she stomped out.

Not one other patient in the rest of that morning surgery mentioned that they had heard anything, but I felt I was being subjected to some very quizzical looks from several of them as they entered the room.

It was a good three months later when Toby himself came to see me, brought in by his mother, for all the world like a cat being taken to the vet.

He had been found guilty and sent to prison for three months. His sentence now over, and having nowhere else to go, he had come home. His grotty little bedsit had soon been occupied by someone else after he had vacated it. He had nowhere to go, other than to his mother.

His mother had given him no chance to explain, no time to tell his story. As far as she was concerned, 'That' was not happening in her family, and she was putting a stop to it. She had enough problems without him starting 'That'.

Toby, not obviously proud of his actions, had come along, to accept whatever the medical profession had in store for him. He was sullen and resentful, and looked as if he could be on the verge of tears, near to a nervous breakdown.

I raised my hand when Mrs Willis, from the depths of the chair into which she had flopped, raised her voice, to get into full flood.

'Not now,' I snapped at her. 'We've been over that before. There is no need to repeat it all.'

Mrs Willis shut her mouth and remained silent. I looked directly at Toby, as he stood unhappily beside his mother. 'Toby, I want to see you alone, to talk. It is going to take at least half an hour. Will you go and see the receptionist, and ask her to book you in, tonight, at the end of surgery?'

He continued to stand there. 'Off you go, now,' I said to him. 'Come back tonight, book the appointment on your way out.'

He walked to the door, and closed it behind him.

'I want him done,' said his mother in her loud voice that must have carried through to the waiting room. 'I'm not putting up with "That".'

I gave Toby a few moments to book his appointment and get away. Mrs Willis was getting into full flood about how she had enough troubles without having to put up with all this nonsense.

Unkindly, I cut her short. 'This is a matter for Toby, and Toby alone,' I told her firmly. 'He's now a grown man of twenty-three, and can make up his own mind. He's got to live his own life now.'

'Right bloody mess he's made of it so far,' she snorted, but she did concede the point, and did not argue.

Reluctantly, she heaved herself out of the chair and went out, off home to shout at Toby or, if he wasn't there, at her sister.

It was a busy day. I was glad to be coming to the end of my evening surgery. I had noticed Toby sitting patiently in the waiting room, and pressed the bell to call him in. It was not Toby who entered, however, but Brian Blotchell, the builder, with a badly squashed and bleeding thumb. Toby had waved him in first.

*   *   *

After I had dressed Brian's shattered thumb, heard how he could not get any extra labour for his big new contract, and told him of Toby's existence, Brian admitted that he was so desperate for extra help, he would take anybody on. He held his painful thumb delicately up in the air.

'It's worse than ever, now, with this,' he said. 'Couldn't have happened at a worse time.'

159

I didn't mention all Toby's other problems.

'He's sitting out there now,' I said. 'He's had a rough time, but I think you'll find he'll come on. I'll send him round to see you tomorrow, shall I?'

'Please,' said Brian. His thumb was painful, and he wanted to go home.

Passing Toby in the waiting room, and holding his injured thumb high in front of him, he nodded to him as he passed.

'Thank you for letting me go in first,' he said. 'I'll see you tomorrow, eight o'clock sharp. At the flats.'

Toby came into the consulting room looking very puzzled.

'What the hell was that all about?' he asked, as he sat down.

'Nothing,' I said. 'We've just fixed you up with a job, starting tomorrow, eight o'clock sharp, at that big block of flats in the High Street. Your duties will be to stand with your foot holding the bottom of the ladder, so that whoever is at the top does not fall down.'

He stared at me, his mouth wide open.

'Better than being castrated, isn't it?' I said.

His mouth remained wide open. Eventually, it shut.

'This isn't a joke?' he said.

'No, far from it. It you take the job you'll be doing him a great favour. He was telling me, while I was sorting out his thumb, that he was desperate for help, and seeing you sitting there, I thought it would do you good as well.'

He sat there, a confusion of conflicting emotions passing over his face.

'You could do with the money?' I said.

'Yes, but . . . '

'Look, seriously, I don't mind if you take the job or not. The only thing is, if you're not going to turn up, will you let him know, then I shan't feel that I've let him down.'

He nodded.

'Think about it, after you leave here, and then let him know.'

He nodded again.

'Now, let's talk about what you really came to see me about.'

The confused emotions were all over his face again. He did not know what to say, where to begin, or even if he wanted to begin. Some things are too private to discuss in cold blood with relative strangers, even if they have been your doctor for ten years.

I sat and waited. If he wanted to tell me, if he felt it would help, he would. I had totally thrown him with Brian's offer of employment.

'You wouldn't really castrate me?' he said eventually.

'Last thing on my mind,' I replied, 'but the first thing on your mother's.'

'Mother . . . ' he said, and I could see he was groping for words. 'Mother . . . ' He looked at me. 'I've got to get out of there. I shall go mad if I stay there.'

'OK,' I said. 'No problem. If you take this job with Brian, with the money you can rent a place of your own.'

He agreed. I waited for him to resume. I did not wish to force him. If he wanted to tell me, he would.

'I don't know whether I'm homosexual or not,' he said, looking directly at me.

'What makes you think you might be?'

'Oh,' he waved his hands in the air. It was not an effeminate wave. 'Never tried the other.' There was a long pause. 'Didn't think much of the gay sort, really, either.'

'What experience have you had?' I asked him gently.

He looked a bit ashamed, a bit guilty.

'If you don't want to tell me, you needn't. Sometimes it helps to talk about it. Sometimes, some things are so private, they're not for talking about.'

I sat and waited.

'It was nothing, really,' he said at last. 'In the remand

161

centre, we mucked about a bit. Didn't really enjoy it. Some of them were real macho, very bad-tempered and frustrated, used to having it regular. One or two were real queens, loved it. Some of them just did it for money. I was in a cell with two of them who did it regular for money, said it was the easiest way they knew of getting any.'

He stopped speaking. I said nothing. A few moments passed by. Inside he was tormented.

'I did it for money,' he said. 'Money for drugs, to escape. The stuff we got inside was bad. I had two real bad trips. I know that if I have another, it'll be so bad I shan't come back. I haven't dared touch it since. I feel dirty inside.'

'Why did you go down to London?' I asked, after he had been silent for a while.

'They were one short,' he said, 'my cellmates from the remand centre. They had this big thing, a real frolic for a visiting party of Arabs. It was all a big set-up. All we did was prance about naked, then the police raided. You can't say you were just having a drink when you've got no clothes on. They were supposed to pay me two hundred quid, but I didn't get anything.'

'What about in prison, after?'

'That was awful. If you're known as a poofter, you can't escape. They're all after you. They seemed to think that the scars on my back were something special. If was easier just to say nothing, and take the money. If you don't co-operate, you get beaten up. Some of them, in for child molesting or raping women, get beaten up regular.'

'What, by the prison staff?'

'No. The prisoners. They can't stand anybody in for rape or doing children. Most of them have to do their time in solitary, or they'd get smashed to bits.'

'Looking back on it, you didn't really enjoy it, then?'

'No, I feel dirty, abused, ashamed. And Mother doesn't help with her ranting and raving about castration. I did feel it might be the best answer. Stop all the bother.'

'Have you ever been with a woman?'

He shook his head negatively.

'Have you ever felt the love of a woman?'

Again he shook his head.

'Promise me one thing,' I said. 'Don't get yourself castrated till you have experienced the love of a real woman, a good woman.'

He smiled, almost laughed.

'You don't think I'm homosexual, then?'

'Not really. Abused, misguided, ignorant, yes; but queer, no.'

'I think I'm going to take that job,' he said quietly. 'You know, all my life, I've been at the bottom of the pile, having things done to me. I thought tonight, before I came in here, I couldn't get any lower. There was nowhere else to go. You know, having a job, and the prospect of a flat, and being able to talk to you, things have cleared. I feel that I'm going to do something, not have it done to me.'

He half-grinned at me. 'All I need is a good woman.'

He rose from his chair.

'There's plenty of them about,' I said.

He walked out of the room.

*　　*　　*

It was September before any more pieces of the jigsaw puzzle were fitted into the picture.

I had seen Brian's thumb on innumerable occasions over the weeks that it had taken to heal. The tip of the bone had been fractured, and the nail-bed had become infected. To a short-handed builder, it had been a very painful, irksome injury. Sometimes he was short-tempered as well as short-handed. The flat renovation did not appear to be going well.

Mrs Blotchell brought the baby to the surgery for the usual post-natal checks, and then on to the baby clinic.

Sometimes they mentioned the two people I had sent to work for them, sometimes not. I assumed that no news was good news, in the sense that if they were working well, they would have no comments to make.

The comments they did make were conversational, in passing, no real news. Neither Margaret nor Toby had been to see me again.

'That Margaret,' Brian said on this particular clear September morning, as I was cleaning the wound yet again. It had been a beautiful autumn morning, a clear blue sky, a crisp frost on the grass, and cock pheasants sparring and fighting all over the farm. I had been up early, first roused from my bed to see a man who could not pass his water, and then on to see Frank get his apple-picking gang organised. The apple I had eaten, crisp with frozen dew, straight off the tree, was delicious. Frank was worrying about the storage conditions, and picking the apples damp.

'That Margaret,' Brian repeated, as I cleaned the crust and plaster dust out of his inflamed and craggy nail-bed, 'She's a close one. Just sits for hours and dreams of you. Did you know?'

'All my female patients sit and dream of me,' I laughed. 'It does my ego good. I sit and dream of them, sitting and dreaming of me. But seriously, one of these days, soon, the right man for her is going to come along, and carry her off.'

'I know,' Brian said. 'I shall be sorry to lose that one. She and the wife get on so well. She minds the baby, does all the books now. She's a good little cook, too. She told the wife all about it, being raped as a child, and how you helped her get over it.'

It was all said so matter-of-factly. The healing process had obviously progressed satisfactorily.

'Each time the wife has come in to see you,' he said, 'she has wanted to talk about it, but didn't.'

'She's a very nice girl,' I said. 'Someday she's going to make some lucky man a damn good wife.'

He grinned at me. 'I know, I only wish I was twenty years younger. No one will get a look in while you're still around. That young Toby, he's really smitten, but he hasn't a chance.'

I grinned back. 'How is young Toby?'

His face became serious. 'When he first started, he was useless. Weak, fidgety, couldn't concentrate. If I went up the ladder, I never knew if the little sod would still be there, at the bottom, with his foot on it. About five times every day, I nearly sacked him, and then I remembered how you said he'd come to, so I just swore at him instead.'

'Did he come to?' I asked. If he was still working there, he must have, I reasoned.

'Took him a damn long time. Do you know what really made him turn the corner?'

'No.' I shook my head.

'Feeding him. Margaret noticed that he was not eating properly, insisted he came and ate with us. Made a world of difference. He seemed to fill out after that. The other thing was putting in the windows.'

He waved his free hand at me. 'I cut this one on some glass – not enough to see you, but sore. With the other out of action, I was no good up the ladder. Toby said he could do it, so I sent him up, and stood on the bottom myself.'

He looked directly at me. 'Do you know, he was like a bleeding monkey. Incredible sense of balance, no fear of heights. He could do in a morning what would have taken me all day.'

'Good,' I said. I finished bandaging his thumb, and he went back to his work.

About two weeks later, unexpectedly, again in the middle of a busy surgery, there was Margaret Chillingford. She was different. More mature, poised, beautiful, but she was crying, pleading for help.

Wordlessly she passed me a letter.

It was a letter written on lined paper, by a hand that was unused to writing. The address was in Birmingham.

Dear Margaret,

This is to let you know that your Mum has passed away. God rest her. I am coming back to live.

Yr Dad

'What do I do?'

'Do you want to see him?'

'No, never, ever.'

'Write and tell him not to come.'

'What if he comes? What if I'm alone, and he jerks his head at me, and makes me go upstairs?'

'Do you think you are strong enough now to say no, and throw him out?'

'I don't know,' she cried. 'I'm so scared. For all those years.'

The tears rolled down her face uncontrollably. 'I don't know, I'm terrified. I don't want to be alone, in case he comes.'

'Have you told Brian and Mrs Blotchell?'

'I can't. I've gone all cold inside again. I can't tell anybody, except you.'

'What about the police? We could tell them.'

She shuddered. 'No, please. Not now, I couldn't face them all over again.'

'The simple answer,' I mused, 'is either for you to go away for a while, or get someone in to live with you, till he's gone away again.'

'I can't go away. My little boy has only just gone to school. I can't disturb him.'

'Who do you know, a friend or a neighbour, who'd move in?'

I waited, hoping that if she'd told the Blotchells, she might well have told others, one of whom could help her.

'The only friend I've got is Toby,' she said at last.

'How do you feel about him? Does he know about you?'

'Toby's sweet,' she said, and there was a long pause. 'I'm very fond of Toby.' She looked up at me, and through the tears came that look, the invitation she had tried not to show. 'I think I'm fond of him as I would be of a brother. I've told him all about my life, and he's told me all about his homosexuality. We have a lot in common, Toby and I. He's a friend, someone to work with.'

She gave me that haunting, longing look again. All the allure of womankind was in it. The look that sent Saint George out after dragons. She knew it affected me.

'What I feel for Toby is not the same as I feel for you. I know I can't have you, but I know that I'll always love you.' The look continued. 'There, I've said it now. I promised myself I never would, but you knew, anyway.'

'Oy, stop that,' I said. 'That's little-girl dreaming again. You love the idea, the vision. The man would be a disappointment.'

I felt relieved that somehow she had said it. We had both been aware of it. In some strange way, it had cleared the air, it was no longer a problem. It was a very similar situation to bringing out into the open her child abuse. She knew that she would always be special to me, too. It was healthy now.

Somehow it made the problem before us a much more practical one. I was beginning to feel that she might be able to cope on her own.

'Would Toby move in with you for a while? Would he behave himself, would you?'

'Would that matter?' For the first time she laughed. For the first time she had considered him as a potential lover, rather than just a probably homosexual friend at work.

She dried her tears and carefully wiped her face. 'I'll tell you what, I'll ask him round to supper tonight, see what he says.' She grinned.

I showed her the door. 'Keep in touch,' I said.

I was certain now that, Toby or no Toby, she could cope with the arrival of her stepfather.

I heard no more. A week must have passed. I presumed that all was well, and was not really thinking about any of them, when Toby's mother, Mrs Willis, heaved her great bulk into my chair. I heard it creak in protest.

A pair of hard, steel-rimmed eyes bored into me.

'Have you done him yet?'

'Pardon?' I said.

'That poncy son of mine, have you had him done yet?'

'Er, no,' I replied, wilting under that look. 'He didn't fancy the operation.'

'Why not? He needed it.'

'We discussed it, and thought it wasn't necessary.'

'Where is he now? In prison again? Never came home since.'

'No, actually, he's not in prison. He's got a good job, and I hear he's got a girlfriend.'

She stared at me in amazement.

'Do you mean to tell me that that poncy little bugger's got a job, earning money, and spending it on some fancy piece, and not bringing his money home like he should?'

'That's how it would appear, Mrs Willis.'

'Was this your doing?'

'I am a doctor, not a job centre.'

'I'll bet you had something to do with it. You tell the poncy little bugger when you see him, that I paid for him for twenty years, and I didn't expect him to walk out on me when he started earning money. You tell him that.'

'I will if I see him, but I haven't seen him since, either.'

She snorted as she heaved herself up, and stalked out.

The next piece of information came from the police. A Mr Chillingford from Birmingham had apparently been beaten senseless by a certain Toby Willis. As far as the police were concerned, it was an apparently motiveless attack. The assault had occurred at the house of his stepdaughter, the house where Mr Chillingford had once lived. Both parties had police records, and both had been in prison. Neither was saying anything, protesting that it was a purely domestic dispute. The only problem was that Mr Chillingford's injuries were somewhat severe: he would be in hospital some considerable time. Toby Willis was merely severely bruised. Could I shed any light on the problem?

'No,' I said. 'I try not to get involved in domestic disputes. Has Miss Chillingford made any statement?'

'Nothing,' said the policeman. 'I ought to charge him with doing Grievous Bodily Harm, but not one of them will say a dicky bird.'

'Perhaps Mr Chillingford started it,' I suggested. 'Perhaps that's why they're not saying anything.'

'Perhaps,' said the policeman.

It took me a long time to find out exactly what had happened.

I made a point, on my next hospital round, of stopping at the bed of Mr Chillingford. From the end of the bed, he looked a very ordinary, nondescript man, with a wispy moustache, grey hair, and a sallow complexion.

The marks of the assault were still on his face. I looked at his records. Toby had been savage and systematic in his beating – one broken arm, one broken leg, and his lower abdomen kicked black and blue. Both his testicles were, according to his notes, swollen and damaged.

He would be in hospital for quite some time.

Versions of what had actually happened varied. Some of the story I gleaned from the police, some Mac picked up from the neighbours. It appeared that Mr Chillingford had arrived with a suitcase. He had called at the local pub, consumed several pints of beer, and enquired after the health and whereabouts of his stepdaughter.

He had been informed that she was still there, had a five-year-old son, and in recent weeks a new boyfriend had appeared, who appeared to be now living in. Swinging his suitcase, he had marched to his old house, knocked loudly on the door, and demanded admission. There had been an altercation on the doorstep, and he had forced an entry.

What happened next had been difficult to ascertain. Both

Margaret and Toby seemed to have developed a healthy sense of privacy about their relationship. It was neither right nor proper to pry, but I did gather from both of them independently that Margaret had been overcome with a great sense of shyness about asking Toby to move in and protect her. He was equally deeply affected. He had moved in, but they lived as brother and sister, thoroughly enjoying each other's company, and both too shy to make the first advance.

That had been the position for the first two weeks. They had virtually concluded that Margaret's letter had deterred her stepfather's visit, when, unannounced, he had barged in.

Toby had been working overtime, Margaret was alone. Drunk, her stepfather had made crude advances. Margaret was trying to beat him off. He had been standing at the foot of the stairs when Toby walked in, and witnessed the jerk of the head, heard the tone of the command 'Upstairs', and saw the look on Margaret's face.

All the pent-up emotions, all the humiliations, all the sorrow of their combined youth seemed to have been exorcised in that beating.

When it was over, they had no desire for revenge, no wish to let the police into a private matter. What was said to Mr Chillingford they never divulged: it was private.

An ambulance had come to take him away. Margaret had thrown his suitcase into the back of it. As far as they were concerned, it was over.

Just before Christmas, Margaret appeared in the surgery. She was radiant, beautiful. All the mystery that was woman was in her face. She smiled at me, and wordlessly gave me another present.

The label read 'From Margaret and Toby'. It was a tie. 'Thank you,' I muttered. I was feeling very emotional.

She gave me that look. 'I'm pregnant,' she said simply.

I arranged all the routine tests.

'We're getting married on January the seventh,' she said. 'Could you wear that tie at our wedding? I'd like you to give me away. Brian Blotchell is best man.' She looked at me. I couldn't speak.

'Will you and your wife be our witnesses?'

I was jelly in her hands. She could have done anything with me.

It was a very simple registry office wedding. There were only the six of us there, and her small son Tony. All three women had tears in their eyes.

After the ceremony, still with the tears shining in her eyes, she held my hands and, with Ruth beaming approval, kissed me full on the lips. All the longing, all the promise, all the mystery of woman was in that kiss. I drowned in it.

'Thank you,' she said, giving me that wonderful, inviting look. She embraced me. Somehow Toby was included in the embrace. I shook hands with him.

'Are you ready for that operation, yet?'

He grinned. They turned to go.

'Keep in touch,' I said.

The last piece of the jigsaw puzzle was in place.

14

Fred, our visiting consultant physician, looked the part. Though normally I never saw him in anything but an impeccably tailored dark blue suit, with striped shirt and club tie, he had come in response to our invitation, a city gentleman, suitably dressed for the countryside.

His almost new Daimler motor car, parked naturally outside our front door, enhanced the image.

Dressed now in green wellington boots, with the obligatory adjustment strap hanging loose, cavalry twill trousers, and tweed jacket worn like a model, he surveyed our acre of rhubarb.

I looked up at the cold grey sky. It had started to drizzle again. Nonchalantly he shrugged himself into his oiled cotton Barbour waterproof. Though shapeless and old, he made it look as if it had been specially styled just for him.

The drizzle of rain reverted to being a torrent. It seemed to have rained non stop for the past two months. Everywhere was soaked, the ground a quagmire of wet mud.

I had compounded the problem by irrigating the rhubarb to saturation just before it had begun to rain in earnest. The few people who had come to pick their own rhubarb stalks had done so in a sea of mud, their footmarks making the whole area akin to the gateway of a field through which a herd of cattle passes twice daily to be milked.

Fred and I squelched delicately into it. It rose up to our ankles.

'Mud,' announced Fred irreverently, as he looked down with distaste at the mud clinging to the legs of his new green wellington boots, 'is essential in the life cycle of the hippopotamus. It keeps their testicles cool in the heat of the breeding season.'

'They should breed well here, then,' I said equally flip-pantly, as I sank into it.

We passed on down the field, to where the stalks had not been stripped so totally, and to where far fewer feet had pulped the soil into such a revolting mess.

'Whatever made you decide to grow rhubarb?' asked Fred, as we surveyed it.

'For the wine-makers, mainly, I suppose,' I answered. 'One of my neighbours saw some growing down in Kent, and was persuaded that it was the one crop with a big future. He assured me that as long as I kept throwing water and nitrogen at it, it kept growing, and the public could keep picking it.'

'Why didn't he grow it himself, then?'

'Because he's a specialist onion grower, and can't handle people picking their own,' I said. 'Though he hates the thought of all those feet trampling over his own land, he talked me into it over a game of billiards.'

'You have obviously,' he remarked, as he elegantly placed his feet into the squelching soil, 'thrown plenty of water and fertiliser at it.'

'I wasn't expecting quite that much rain,' I admitted.

We walked further down the edge of the rows. The stalks of rhubarb were at least two feet all, and the leaves the size of modest unbrellas.

'It's supposed to be the earliest Pick Your Own crop there is, being ready before the gooseberries and the straw-berries,' I told him. 'And then after the early growth, the wine-makers can move in during the summer, and pick it all the year. In theory, it's very profitable, but . . .' I shrugged my shoulders to indicate the mess and waste around us. To date it hadn't taken enough money to pay for the original plants, and was now in its third year.

'My old grandfather,' said Fred, stopping to point out an enormous plant which was nearly twice the size of any other around it, 'I remember him well. He used to make rhubarb wine. It was in the days of horses and carts, of course. He used to get all his visitors blind drunk on it, put them in the cart, and then send the horse home with a good smack on its behind.'

He reached into the plant and brought out a long white, thick, succulent stick. He surveyed it with distaste.

'This was the sort. Great big ugly pale stuff. I remember the time when I used to have to help him make it. We would strip the leaves off out in the garden, and then put the stalks through the mangle. The juice from this was a smelly, watery green. We had to put in some of the stalks from the red sort to give it a bit of colour.'

He shuddered, and threw the stalk down into the mud.

'My job,' he continued, 'was to turn the handle of the mangle. Grandfather fed in the stalks. The juice dripped down into Grandmother's tin washing tub.'

He stopped, turned and looked at me. 'Do you know, that stuff was so acid it ate the galvanising off Grandmother's tin bath.'

'I can believe it,' I said.

"The smell was quite revolting as it fermented,' he remembered. 'I can picture it still. The juice turned a dirty grey colour, with a scum on the top. After a while it cleared, and all the greyness settled out as a sediment. Once that had happened, Grandfather bottled it.'

We walked a little further down the field.

'Did you ever drink any of it?' I asked.

'Good God, no,' he laughed. 'Grandfather never gave any of it to his family or real friends. He saved it for those people he had to entertain – neighbours, and business acquaintances.' He laughed again. 'He said it made them more amenable, before they passed out. It was very potent stuff.'

'I remember my mother telling me a similar story,' I said. 'She remembers her father making it. It had to be kept for seven years, and then it was as potent as whisky.'

174

'Yes,' he said. 'There was a definite social message when Grandfather produced the rhubarb wine. Real friends had his special or Christmas cider. That was very special.'

He needed no urging to tell me all about it. The main orchard of cox's apples was next to the rhubarb. He waved his arms in the general direction of the trees.

'You know, ordinary cider is from the juice of fresh apples. The apples are mashed up, and then the juice squeezed out in an enormous press.'

'Yes,' I said.

'Well,' he continued, 'for his special cider Grandfather put the apples in a two-bushel wheat sack, and just left the sacks in a corner to rot.'

'Didn't all the juice run out?' I asked.

'Didn't seem to, not if the sacks weren't moved. When he wanted some special, he put a sack through the mangle, and bottled the juice straight away.'

'Didn't the bottles explode as the juice fermented?' I asked.

'Some did,' he replied, 'but he used mainly either old lemonade or beer bottles, those with a dent in the bottoms. Only a few did, and it was a very impressive bang, I remember, with slivers of glass stuck in the ceiling, and Grandmother having hysterics in the kitchen. I suppose most of the fermentation had occurred in the sacks. There was only enough nutrient left to give a champagne-like fizz to it. It was marvellous stuff, I remember, very like champagne.'

He laughed. 'You know, I haven't thought of my grandparents for years, but the thing that I remember most vividly about them is cleaning the mangle afterwards.' He shook his head. 'It was the same mangle that Grandma used every week for her washing. She used to get so mad every time he used it. No matter how hard it was scrubbed, and how much we rinsed it, Grandma always complained, for weeks afterwards, that her washing came out sticky.'

We continued to the bottom of the rhubarb patch, and looked back up the hill.

'What variety are they?' he asked, waving his hand at the plants.

'They're supposed to be "Timperly Early",' I replied, 'but either we've got a remainder job lot, or all that fertiliser we put on in the spring has been washed into the roots of just a few plants. Just look at them, there's no two the same.

'Suits the public, though,' I went on. 'Last year was the first time we let them onto the bed to pick their own. Some of them want all long thin red ones, others only go for the short fat white ones.'

We turned round, and retraced our steps back up the field.

'You can see,' I pointed out, 'how everyone wants a stalk off the first plant they come to. No one wants to walk down to the bottom of the field, even if the crop is much better there. The top is nearly stripped bald, trodden into a muddy mess, and the bottom has hardly a leaf gone, or a footprint in it.'

The rain increased. We turned up the collars of our waterproofs and plodded on, up the mud.

'Surely,' Fred said, after a while, 'you force rhubarb, bring it on early, and all that.'

'We tried that last year,' I told him. 'What you're supposed to do is dig up the roots in the autumn, and let the frost get well into them. This makes them think they've had a winter. Then, at Christmas time, you bring the roots into the warm and the dark. They think it's spring, and sprout out all over the place. The darkness makes the stalks long and tender.'

'Didn't it work?' he asked.

'Not the way we did it,' I replied. 'I thought that if we placed straw bales all down the rows between the plants, and then covered them up with loose straw, this would protect them from the cold, and they would sprout early.'

'What happened, then?'

'Well, first they didn't get a proper winter. They just sat

176

there, sending out a few weak and feeble little shoots, to test the going, so to speak. When the spring did come, all that insulating straw stopped the soil from warming up, and all we got were a few more weak and feeble little shoots about the size of tulip stalks, and about as much use. The rhubarb took a whole year to get over the experience.'

'Not very profitable,' he said, continuing to plod up the field. We had now reached the part where many feet had ploughed it into a real mess.

'No,' I agreed. 'Got any idea what we can do with it?'

He did not answer as we struggled on, by mutual consent heading for home, and warmth.

'I'll think of something,' he said eventually.

The rain, previously gusting intermittently, had now set into a steady downpour. There seemed little pleasure in continuing on our tour of inspection of the fruit farm. I merely pointed out the various crops and features as we returned to the house.

The invitation to Fred had been a combination of business and pleasure. He had come, first to lunch and a walk round the farm, and then secondly to see a patient on a domiciliary visit. We both knew that there was not a lot he could do; it was more a gesture of moral support.

We returned to the safety of a warm kitchen and hot tea. Wet and muddy coats and boots had been hung to dry.

'Tell me about your patient, all over again,' said Fred, reaching for his steaming cup. 'I don't suppose that I will be any more help than I have with the rhubarb, but we must be seen to try.'

There was little to tell him. Medically, it was very simple; the complications were social.

Mrs Ella White, the widow of Joshua White, was an aged, but loved matriarch. Now eighty-one, for the previous fifty years she had ruled over a turbulent family of four sons and their squabbling wives. She now had fourteen grandchildren, and claimed that she had lost count of the great-grandchildren, as they came so fast she couldn't keep up with them. Her husband had died relatively young, leaving her the farm.

During the course of those fifty years, the family had worked hard, and had prospered. As more members had grown up, and had naturally joined the workforce, so, naturally, had more land been acquired for them to work. Some of this land had been rented, but the bulk of it had been purchased, on assorted forms of agricultural mortgages.

There was now a considerable farming and financial empire, scattered all over the county, and nominally all owned by Mrs Ella White.

Mrs White had kept the ownership in her own name for all these years for one very simple reason. Though she appeared to love her daughters-in-law, she knew they did not love each other. Had any one of them the power to do so, they would have separated from the other three years ago, scattering the whole enterprise into fragments.

As the farms and the empire had grown in size, she had kept the peace by keeping them apart. It was a sort of Pax Britannica. No one of them could possibly leave the fold, or challenge for supreme position, while Mrs Ella White still ruled.

It had been pointed out to her, on innumerable occasions, that on her death the demands of the taxman for estate duty would virtually eat up the whole enterprise, rendering most of her descendants penniless. Her sons were only too aware of the problem.

Her answer had always been that she wished to consolidate the whole, and when it was big and solid enough to divide, she would do so.

Grandly, at the age of seventy-five, she had deemed it safe enough to be distributed, and handed it over to her sons, in equal parts. Gracefully, the daughters-in-law had each taken their share, and retired to their own farms. Now that they no longer had to pretend to like each other, their relationships had become much easier.

The problem was that Mrs Ella White was obliged to live for seven years after the transfer. If she did not, most of her estate would still be taken in death duties.

Now, in her eighty-second year, with only six months of the seven years to go, she had suffered a brain haemorrhage.

Over tea in the kitchen, I told Fred all about her health, and how it now appeared that she had left her tax avoidance scheme a few months too late. I also told him that it was her eldest son, Tom, the onion specialist, who had initially persuaded me to grow rhubarb. The tea consumed, Fred and I set off to meet him. It had stopped raining.

Tom, accompanied by all the daughters-in-law, formed a reception committee as Fred and I emerged from the Daimler and walked up to the front door of the old original farmhouse where Mrs Ella still lived. She lived here, alone, with only her daily help, Doris, in irregular attendance.

In strict order of precedence, Fred was introduced to the family. As if meeting royalty, each gave a slight, but dignified bow. After all, it was not every day that such a man of presence and culture was escorted into their house.

Like royalty, Fred returned the greeting. To receive such deference was natural to him.

In procession we entered the house, and were ushered into the bedroom of the comatose matriarch.

I had already given Fred a full history of the incident, of how she had been found unconscious on the floor by the daily help, after having complained of the sudden and severe onset of a headache. Over lunch, we had both agreed it was an absolutely classic presentation of a sub-arachnoid haemorrhage, the leaking of a small artery into the fluid surrounding the brain, not into the brain itself.

The daily help had been quite emphatic.

'There she was,' she said, 'standing at the kitchen sink,

as usual.' She drew herself up to her full height. 'We were washing up,' she explained. 'Suddenly she said to me, "Doris," she said, "something has just hit me on the back of my neck." I looked all round, but there was only me and her there, and nothing had hit her. "Yes, ma'am," I said to her. You didn't argue with Mrs Ella.'

I had agreed, you didn't argue with Mrs Ella.

'And then,' the daily help had continued, 'she just folded up, like, and fell on the floor.'

By the time that I had arrived, the family had gathered, carried her up to her bed, and all four daughters-in-law had undressed her and attired her in her nightclothes.

Very professionally, she had been laid in the left lateral position. In this position, lying on the left side, with the upper arm and leg pointing forward, the almost inevitable vomiting of an unconscious patient is not dangerous. An unconscious patient, lying on her back, will inhale and drown in her own vomit.

I had forgotten that the wife of Tom, the onion grower, had once been a ward sister. Quite naturally, she had assumed the mantle of responsibility of her mother-in-law's nursing, and quite naturally the other wives had followed her lead.

I had examined Mrs Ella very carefully. All her limbs were slightly spastic, and her neck was totally rigid, the classic sign of irritation of the surface of the brain.

'It is a subarachnoid haemorrhage, I presume?' Tom's wife had informed me tactfully.

'Yes,' I had agreed.

The problem was what to do about it. I discussed it with the family.

Ideally, an unconscious patient should be in hospital, but if the bleeding has stopped naturally, the movement of the ambulance journey could very well restart it. To confirm the diagnosis, I should really perform a lumbar puncture – that is, insert a long needle into the subarachnoid space and confirm the presence of blood, but to do this, soon after a fresh bleed, could also cause the bleeding to start again. There was a very strong case for doing absolutely nothing.

'At the age of eighty-one,' I had told them, 'I think that the best treatment is not to disturb her, and to nurse her at home, if you can all cope.'

The nursing sister had agreed, and the others had no option but to follow, though doubts were expressed.

'Wouldn't the best treatment be to get her into hospital, and perform an operation to stop the bleeding?' asked the youngest, and hence most junior wife.

'Of course,' I agreed, 'but there's a very high chance that even moving her into hospital could kill her.'

I had explained to them that even if I admitted her to hospital and referred her to the neurosurgeons with a view to operating, they would not contemplate it for at least six weeks, until this acute episode had thoroughly settled down. Operative interference before this time usually caused more problems than it solved.

Thus had the matter rested for the first few days. Mrs Ella had developed a swallowing reflex, so that with careful and diligent application of a feeding cup, sufficient fluid had been taken in. If she had been unable to swallow, then hospital, with all the risk of getting her there, would have been necessary, in order to set up an intravenous drip and give her the vital fluid into a vein.

A catheter had been inserted into her bladder, so that she should not wet the bed. Her nursing care had been exemplary, faultless. There were no bedsores at all, she remained well hydrated, and her lungs remained free from congestion and infection.

Everything was going extremely well, except for the fact that she showed not the slightest sign of returning consciousness.

Despite my repeated assurance that she could take up to six or more weeks to improve, we were all getting a bit apprehensive. I had asked Fred to give us his professional opinion as to whether we should continue, or whether the time had come to move the old lady into hospital.

On a domiciliary visit, Fred was impressive. After one of his performances, even if the prognosis was hopeless, the spirits of both the patient and the relatives were always lifted.

I could but admire his technique as he questioned them all, extracting all the minute details of the story, exhorting and thanking each in turn.

Thus fully informed, Fred began to examine the patient. He demonstrated her very stiff neck, her increased reflexes, and listened very assiduously to her chest.

Replacing his stethoscope in his pocket, he opened up the case of his ophthalmoscope, and screwed the component parts together.

Elegantly, he knelt on the floor and, pulling up each eyelid in turn, peered into the backs of her eyes, to see with his instrument the retinal arteries as they ran in full view across the back of the eye.

'Beautiful,' he said to himself. 'Beautiful.' He gazed at the assembled company, hanging on his every word. 'Those are the blood vessels of a young woman. She will live for years yet.'

Carefully, he replaced all his equipment in his case.

'Tell me,' he said, looking directly at Tom, 'you're the one who misguidedly persuaded Dr Jackson here to grow rhubarb on his fruit farm.'

'Well, yes,' Tom replied, looking like an embarrassed schoolboy confronted unexpectedly by the headmaster.

Fred continued to gaze directly at him.

'Why did you persuade him to grow that odd job lot of "Timperly Early"?' he asked.

Tom shrugged. All he had done was show me the advertisement for the crowns in the *Grower* magazine.

Fred continued to talk about rhubarb. He sounded very

182

knowledgeable as he repeated all I had told him about the crop a few hours ago. The family were most impressed, as irrigation amounts and nitrogen levels were casually dropped.

In procession, still talking rhubarb, we moved downstairs to the dining-room, where ceremonial tea and biscuits awaited.

When Fred came to the end of his discussion, and I realised that he now had nothing further to say about rhubarb, I asked the question on all their minds.

'What do we do about Grandma?'

'Oh, carry on,' he said imperiously. 'You're all doing a marvellous job. I agree that hospital is definitely not the place for her.' He did not mention the potential death duty liability, merely waved his hands expressively.

'She'll live to be a hundred, mark my words. Keep up the good work.'

He leaned across the table to Tom.

'Tell me,' he said, 'while I'm here, where I'm going wrong with my onions.' And very skilfully, in a series of brilliantly simple questions, he elicited from him the basics of commercial onion growing.

'Much more profitable than rhubarb,' he commented. Somewhere, sometime, in the near future. Fred would impress someone enormously with the depth of his knowledge and experience of onion growing.

I noticed Tom's wife slip away from the table and return with a cardboard box. In it was a bottle wrapped in tissue paper. She presented it to him.

'I know Mother-in-law would like you to have this,' she said. 'She keeps it for her special guests. She would have enjoyed your visit.'

Gravely Fred thanked her and, carrying the bottle and his bag, we proceeded in procession to his car.

The bottle contained twelve-year-old rhubarb wine.

Fred thought for a moment. 'I wonder if she knew my grandfather,' he said.

Still smiling, we drove back home. The rain had resumed. A grey sky was positively emptying itself over us. We drew up outside the front door and I waited for a pause in the downpour. After a few moments, it eased up a little. I prepared to get out. As I opened the car door, Fred leaned over towards me. 'I think I have the answer to your mud and rhubarb problem,' he said.

I looked at him enquiringly. As far as I was concerned, it was a total dead loss.

'Import a pair of hippopotamuses,' he said. 'They can wallow in the mud while they eat all that rhubarb. In a couple of years, you can organise a safari to shoot your own hippo meat.'

'Yes,' I said, as I ran in out of the rain.

True to prediction, Mrs Ella started to recover almost the next morning. Fred's visit had been very therapeutic. I never did ask him what happened to the rhubarb wine.

15

Routinely, I pressed the bell for the next patient. It was one of those dark winter surgeries, when the sun has never penetrated the clouds, the rain is thrown in all directions by the wind, and the patients are cold, wet and uncommunicative. They hurry in and out of the surgery as quickly as possible, in order to get back home – home to a warm fire, and home to get the medication inside them.

Only wildfowlers enjoy such weather, when the ducks fly fast and low across the wind, in and out of range in a flash.

It was the weather and the season for the wigeon, Arctic ducks that migrate south for the winter and congregate in huge flocks on the flat, muddy shores of tidal estuaries. Gorgeous little brown and white birds that call to each other with a haunting, evocative whistle.

I had brought a whole clutch of these wigeon as eggs, home from Iceland. They had hatched in my shirt and been reared by hand. Quite categorically never for sale, they had thrived, mated with the other wigeon in the collection, and formed a fair flock.

We would lie in bed, hearing the gales lash the rain against the side of the house, and listen to our wigeon whistling into the wind.

All that morning I had listened to them. In my imagination, I could hear them in the wind outside my surgery window.

The next patient walked in through the open door.

Her face was a mask, frozen, expressionless, any feeling or emotion totally hidden. Other than that she was a beautiful woman. Not young, but young enough still to have attraction and, but for the wooden face, graceful, as she walked across the surgery floor to the waiting chair.

'Good morning,' I said routinely, as I reached for her folder of notes. I had never met her before, and the single card of records was blank, with only today's date on its blue-lined page. She had only registered with us as a patient that morning.

I glanced up from her non-informative records to her face. The fixed mask of control gazed evenly back. 'Mrs Overton?' I said, to break the ice. 'Mrs Grace Overton?'

'Yes,' she said. 'That's right.'

I waited, but she didn't speak.

'Tell me about it,' I said.

'It's my throat,' she said. 'It's been sore for several months, and just won't get better.' There was a slight pause, a hint of unease. 'I'm sorry to bother you with it.'

Tonsillitis is one of the things that is always with us. Little epidemics of it flow to and fro across the schools, spreading ripples of infection out into the community. We were in the midst of such an epidemic now.

Sometimes this tonsillitis can become chronic, a painful nuisance that the patient hopes will get better tomorrow. Busy, active people tend to put off seeing doctors until they are desperate, and then feel embarrassed for coming with something so trivial.

I assumed that she was just another case of chronic tonsillitis, needing a course of penicillin, and that her tense, wooden expression was just a manifestation of a nervous person seeing a strange doctor for the first time. It was not unusual.

I rose from my chair and walked the two paces to her. I tried to put her at her ease.

'Open wide, and say "Ah",' I said routinely.

Taking a spatula and pushing her tongue down with one hand, I shone my torch down into the back of her throat. Her mouth had opened wide to expose it, with the prac-

186

tised ease of the worried hypochondriac. There was singularly little to see: old healed scarring of the tonsillar bed where the tonsils had been removed in her youth, a mild catarrhal pinkness of the rest of the pharynx, but otherwise absolute normality.

I inspected her ear drums, and felt for glands in her neck, all utterly normal, but the muscle tension in her neck and shoulders was extreme. Her masked face was hiding considerable anxiety.

'Does it only hurt when you swallow, or all the time?' I asked.

Genuinely inflamed throats are usually bearable at rest, but very painful on attempting to swallow.

A continuous pain in the throat, not related to swallowing, is not usually due to an infection, a tonsillitis, but is much more often a reflection of an inner state of tension. The tense, taut muscles ache with fatigue, the fatigue of emotional exhaustion.

The fact that the throat aches, and is sore, sends the patients to their doctors. The fact that the doctors can find nothing wrong does not reassure the patients, merely convinces them that there is something unknown and sinister going on.

They worry because it hurts; it hurts because they worry, and so the vicious circle goes on.

To attempt to treat the throat with anaesthetic sprays is temporary palliation, something to do, while the real cause of the tension is exposed.

I waited for her answer.

'It hurts all the time,' she said. 'It feels as if I've got a huge aching lump sitting there.'

I walked round behind her, as she sat, tense and rigid, in the chair, and put my hands on her neck again.

The muscles to her shoulders were still tense and hard, as tense as the guy ropes on a scout tent in the rain.

Massaging gently as I examined them again, I said in a soft voice,

'You are a very tense person, aren't you?' and as I moved her neck backwards and forwards, 'Come on, relax.'

It took a while, but slowly those knotted muscles softened.

'Does that feel better?' I asked as I resumed my seat.

'Yes,' she nodded.

'You're tense all over, aren't you?' I said, more of a statement than a question.

Again, she nodded agreement.

'Your neck muscles,' I said, observing just the slightest weakening of that frozen mask, 'are like the rest of you, so tense and strung up, I could almost pluck them, like guitar strings.'

Her eyes admitted it.

'Your throat,' I said, 'is a tube, a hollow tube made of muscles, and lined with special skin.'

There was again the slightest nod of agreement.

'If the muscles in this tube contract, the tube becomes smaller, and the lining skin folds up and wrinkles inside it.'

She was listening with attention.

'One wrinkle touches another wrinkle, and if there is the slightest bit of catarrhal inflamation, each slightly swollen wrinkle sends out the message that there's something touching it. All these small messages from all these small wrinkles add up to the feeling that there's a huge lump there, don't they?'

I paused. She nodded agreement.

'Not only that, those tense muscles ache, don't they?'

We sat and looked at each other for several moments.

'This has been going on for several months,' I said. 'What's the underlying problem, what's really the matter? Do you want to talk about it?'

Thirty seconds can seem like an eternity.

'A year ago today,' she said slowly and softly, 'my mother committed suicide. She took her own life. She hated the cold weather, hated the winter, hated cold, wet water, yet on the coldest day of the year, when it was pouring with rain, she walked out of her house and, it seems, threw herself into the river.'

I waited. There was obviously much more to come. Much more than thirty seconds passed.

Sooner or later, she would start to cry, and once she started, it would become uncontrollable, releasing, as she wept, all that bottled up emotion. I had seen it all too often before.

Emotion expressed is healthy. It cleans the interior wounds, releases the tensions, and initiates the healing process. Emotion hidden behind the stiff upper lip festers like an abscess, building up over time to actual psychotic states, or it comes out in psychosomatic illnesses such as asthma, dermatitis, stomach ulcers, and so on. In this case it had just produced the chronic tension state, the incurable sore throat, and the pains in the neck.

Mac had been taught by a generation of physicians who called this syndrome 'fibrositis', as the chronic tensions in the muscles of the neck could be felt as knotted and fibrous lumps. The attention given to these knotted muscles, in the form of heat, massage, and all the soothing balms, only really relaxed the outward tensions. The time given, and the sympathy involved in applying the remedy, were the real cure.

There is no cure for death, only consolation for the bereaved. This takes many forms, from the sympathetic shoulder of a friend to cry on, right up to all the more formal rites of state and religion.

Where grief is inconsolable, the expression of emotion often makes it easier to bear. The acceptance of the death is the first step in overcoming the situation.

To give consolation effectively is difficult, and in many instances impossible. There is insufficient time, and in many cases, the tragedy is too fresh for any form of comfort to be received. Often, in a gesture more of sympathy than therapeutic efficiency, the only positive response of any doctor is the ritual prescription of a sedative; where this is the only consolation, and the grief remains unexpressed, bottled up until a state of real depression is reached, then trouble is usually ahead.

Repeated bottles of pills merely put a barrier between the emotion and its expression. They may in the short term be all that one has to offer, but in the long term it is often better to spend more time exposing the problem at the first consultation.

I sat and waited for the flood gates to open.

She cried and spoke incoherently. I passed her a box of tissues. 'For five days,' she said, addressing the paper handkerchief clutched in her lap, 'for five whole days, the police questioned me as to where she was, where I'd put the body.'

She looked up at me, the resentment, the anger, the bitterness, the hopelessness, all showing on her face. 'I was desperate,' she said. 'I was worried sick. Mother had never spent even one night away from home. She hated the rain, she was frightened of the dark, she never went out alone.'

'Go on,' I said, when she paused.

'Mother was nervous, quiet, never answered anybody back. She couldn't stand the winters; she'd get a good fire on in the afternoon, lock the doors, and not go out again.'

'Did you live with her?' I asked, after a longish pause.

'Only after my divorce,' she said. 'Before that I had a home of my own, but it didn't work. We were one of the couples who never should have married, but it took us ten years to find out.'

She stopped speaking, not looking at my face.

'Tell me more about your mother,' I said, into the silence.

'Not a lot to tell,' she said evenly. 'Mother hated living down there on that Essex coast, but that's where Father worked. Perhaps, like us, they should have got divorced years ago, not just kept going, out of habit.

190

'It's all mud down there. No sand. The tide goes out for ever.'

In my mind I could picture it. The mud flats stretching out towards the sea, in the far distance. On the flats were the little channels, like the veins on a leaf, where the water rushed up and down as the tide changed – empty and safe one moment, several feet deep, and full of racing water the next. Dangerous to those who do not know and respect them. A place where the wigeon fly and whistle to each other.

But she did not see the salt marshes like that, she saw them as cold, wet, muddy and desolate places. A place to go to commit sucicide.

'Why did she do it?' I asked.

'*If* she did,' Mrs Overton said quietly.

I waited for her to continue. She wiped her eyes with a tissue and, with an effort, seemed to compose herself.

'My mother did not have a happy life. She hated the place, but was trapped in it, if you know what I mean.'

She looked at me. I understood.

'If she had left, she had no money, no home, no job. Father did not earn a lot, barely enough for the housekeeping.'

I nodded. It was not a unique situation.

'They lived together by necessity. There was no love, no feeling. It was like two lodgers staying in the same boarding house, or two people who work at adjoining benches in a factory – you know what I mean?'

I did. I knew what she meant.

'I got married to get away from it: the emptiness, the pointlessness, the indifferent silence.'

She paused.

'My marriage was just as bad. Once the excitement of going away was past, he had his work, I had mine, we went straight down the same road as my parents. I lived alone for a while, lost my job, went back home.'

There was a longer silence, while she fiddled with the paper tissues.

'Mother and I understood each other. It took us a long time to be able to put it into words, but we understood. I was closer to her just before she died than ever before. If she was going to kill herself, she'd have told me.'

She looked across the desk straight at me. 'It's the truth, honest to God,' the agony coming through in her voice. 'I'd have known if she was going to kill herself.'

'What happened?' I asked.

'I don't know,' she cried. 'I don't know. I'd been out all day. I'd been depressed, worried, out of work, and I just went out, walked, shops, getting away. When I came home, late and tired, Mother wasn't there.'

She looked at me again.

'Go on,' I said.

'Father had reported us missing to the police. He'd come home, empty house, no supper. The police were there, asking questions: What had I done with her? Where was she? As if I'd murdered her.'

There was another long pause.

'When they'd gone, he just sat there, reading his paper.'
She glared her indignation at me.

'For five days those policemen came. Questions. Questions. Questions. Always the same: Who'd seen me? Where had I been? What had I done with her?'

She paused again, and slumped a little in her chair.

'And all the time he just sat there, reading his paper.'

She sat a little higher in the chair, and then slumped down again. Resignation, acceptance, on her face.

'They found her body washed up in the estuary.'

'Then what happened?' I asked gently. I did not wish to intrude, but felt that there was much more to come.

'The inquest was "Suicide while the balance of the mind", and all that. The police had suspected me of God knows what, but too many people had seen me wandering round the town.'

There was more to come, I waited for it.

'When the inquest was over, Father produced his girl-friend. They'd had an affair for twenty years. Mother must have known, but never said a word. It seems he was at her house when Mother went missing, at least that's what they told the police. She moved in. I wasn't wanted.'

I felt there was still more to come.

'Go on,' I said after a while.

She looked up at me before she spoke.

'About six months ago, things had got intolerable. No one was speaking in that house. Father said, one evening, he wanted to talk. To walk and talk.

'We got in his car, and drove right down to the estuary, where the wildfowlers go. The tide was right out and we walked to the sea. He said he was sorry. The tide started to come in. One of those streams cut us off.'

She paused again.

'That's when I knew for certain,' she said sadly. 'Every-body round there knows that if you get cut off by the tide coming in fast up a stream, you walk north, to get above it. He tried to persuade me to run south, where it would be shallower, while he waded through it there.'

She looked at me intently.

'Mother wouldn't have known that. She hated the place. Hated the cold and the wet. I knew then, and he knew that I knew: he'd brought her down there that evening for a chat, let her panic, and told her to run south. She just ran into the tide.'

I tried to take in what she was saying.

'It was murder,' she said. 'Cold-blooded, premeditated murder.'

Her face had cleared. She looked calmer.

'What did you do, then?'

'I ran north, and I've never been back. He doesn't know whether I ran into the sea or not.'

'Have you told anyone else?' I asked.

'No,' she said. 'I really still can't believe it myself, but it's true. For six months I've known it, but couldn't believe it. My father murdered my mother, and I've got to live with it.'

'Can you live with it?' I asked, after a while.

'I don't know,' she said.

We waited silently for a while, and she rose to go.

'You're right about my throat,' she said.

'If I can be of any help,' I said, 'I'm here.'

'Thank you,' she said.

She went out of the door. In the silence after she had gone, I could hear the rain and the wind.

I could imagine that lonely foreshore, hear the wigeon whistling.

I sat down.

I never saw her again. Like a migrant wigeon, she had flashed within range out of the storm, whistled into the wind, and flown away.

16

I was not really surprised when Rupert handed in his notice. He said that he did not fancy a winter pruning apples, for after all, he was now a fully qualified tractor driver. As such he had got another job.

He had my sympathy. I would not have looked forward to the whole of the winter, sunshine or rain, frost or snow, outside the entire time, cutting out branches with saw and secateurs.

I think, too, that the old guard had quietly encouraged him to move on, more by what had not been said than by verbal communication.

Absolutely nothing had been said to me by anyone, after the incident of the crow. Nothing at all. Sylvester Jones had not been to see me, Moira had just stopped being part of the workforce.

It was as if she had never been. Her name was no longer on the list of casuals, and nobody remarked on it. It was as if her name had been struck from the collective memory, by the thought police.

That first payday after the incident, Rupert had appeared with a somewhat large and tender nose, and a magnificent pair of black eyes. I had enquired tactlessly how it had happened.

'Branch sprung back at me, on a tree,' he had muttered sullenly, and I had not pursued the matter.

Sylvester Jones's seventy-year-old predecessor as chief clerk at Thorpe and Goodman, the solicitors, rubbed his hands together in glee as he sat in the surgery chair having his blood pressure taken, and reported village gossip of the incident.

Apparently Sylvester had been skinning the crow on the kitchen table when Moira had arrived home, semi-nude, distraught, and covered from head to foot with a blistering rash from her passage through the stinging nettles.

Sylvester had been too busy inside his crow to notice her appearance as she rushed in and headed for the stairs. She, however, had seen the crow, and assuming that Sylvester had at least been involved in the shooting of it, had gone quite hysterical.

After a row that had apparently been overheard by several corroborative witnesses, Sylvester, armed with his partially skinned crow, had gone to seek out Rupert.

'I'll give him his due,' the old man had cackled. 'He might be a jumped up little toad from London, but he's a wicked little bastard when he's riled.'

There had been other witnesses to the fight. It had not been all one-sided, but righteous anger and indignation had triumphed over adulterous guilt, I had gathered from several sources.

Sylvester resigned from his job and returned to London. Moira went with him, leaving large 'For Sale' notices all over their cottage.

The elderly retired solicitors' managing clerk reported triumphantly back to his ex-employers, offering his services, if only on a temporary basis, and was deeply offended when his offer was declined.

I do not know what became of the crow. Its corpse was lost somewhere along the way.

Rupert had stayed till Christmas, given us a week's notice, and moved on. Gossip reported that he had gone back to his home territory in the Midlands.

Once more we were short of a tractor driver, but Frank hinted that he could manage till spring, if Joe or I gave him an occasional hand.

We had all gathered for the first meeting of the new year, to try to establish the course of action for the following spring.

It was a Sunday morning, cold and raw. Ruth had lit the fire through in my study.

In an old farmhouse such as ours, the kitchen is invariably the warmest place in the house. The heat from the old solid fuel Aga cooker warms the atmosphere, as well as the walls, and the kettle sings on the hob. Coffee is but a hand-stretch away. The whole room invites and welcomes, particularly if enticing aromas of roasting meat, or baking bread, are coming from the ovens. It is the centre, the heart of the house, particularly if Ruth is in it.

The entrance to the house is the back door, into the kitchen. Boots can be kicked off in the porch, and worn old work trousers do not mark and spoil wooden kitchen chairs.

Edmund Franklin had been the first to arrive. As Ruth had seen his car come up the drive, she turned from the sink, where she was washing a saucepan.

'I'm not having them all in here while I'm trying to cook a meal,' she warned.

'I know,' I said. 'I'll take them all through into the study.'

'I realise,' she said, 'that it is one of the crosses I have to bear, to have the misfortune to have to cook in the farm office, but do you think, just for today, that you could mean it when you say you'll have the meeting in your study, so that I can cook lunch in peace?'

I agreed that I could. I would take them all straight through into my study, as they arrived.

Edmund tapped gently on the door, pushing it open as he did so.

'Can I come in?'

He smiled a diffident greeting at Ruth, nodded at me and, with accustomed familiarity, sat down at the table.

'Coffee?' asked Ruth, out of force of habit.

'Please,' he said, reaching for the cup she passed to him.

'Do you think,' he said quietly, 'that before everyone else gets here, you could write a prescription for some more of my pills?'

'Of course,' I agreed. Ever since his stay in hospital, he had required various medicaments. As long as he took them, he remained in perfect health.

I walked to my study to fetch a prescription pad, placed it on the kitchen table and wrote it out for him.

'Thanks,' he said. 'While you're at it, could you do one for Rose as well?'

Rose was his wife, who suffered from mild hypertension and a slight anxiety state. She needed some Beta blockers. I had recently checked her blood pressure, so wrote out the prescription and passed it to him.

We heard Bob coming up the drive. Ruth automatically poured more coffee. He came in. Edmund and I looked at each other and smiled in relief. He had a hat on – only a small one, but a hat, a very dapper little trilby. He was on the up.

He seated himself at the table, saw the prescription pad, and said, 'Yes. I was going to ask you. Can you do one for me for both the Lithium and the Tryptizol?'

I picked up my pen. I had barely written his name and address on the top, when the phone rang.

Ruth answered it in the hall.

She poked her head round the door. 'It's for you,' she said.

Reluctantly I rose from my chair and walked over to the phone.

'Hello?' I said slowly. It was my weekend off, for both practice and hospital. Both were adept at catching me: 'I know you're not on duty, but . . . '

Once I had been landed with the problem, I had no option but to deal with it. Ruth managed to fend off most of these requests, unless they were screaming obstetric emergencies, but as our little unit had got bigger and busier, these emergencies happened ever more frequently.

'Sorry to bother you,' said the voice out of the instrument. It was a voice I didn't instantly recognise. 'But can you sign my application to renew my shotgun certificate?'

I recognised the voice: it was Kenneth Woodman, patient and enemy, the farm safety officer. As a patient, he was quite a reasonable man. As the farm safety officer, he was a pain in our collective necks.

According to his little blue book of rules, most of our machinery was obsolete and dangerous. The various guards on the power take-off shafts on the tractors were worn out, so that virtually everything that we possessed had been condemned by him.

This was a situation inherited from Sir Percy. About every three months he came on a ceremonial inspection, to see just what we had corrected since his last visit. So far, we had managed to keep him fairly satisfied.

Sir Percy had given me invaluable advice on how to deal with such persons, be they safety officers, VAT inspectors, taxmen, or what.

'Give the b – – – – – s some rabbits to shoot at.'

I had expressed bewilderment.

'It's like this,' he had explained. 'If you go out to a farm, on a shoot, and as you start, pheasants fly up from under your feet, partridges whistle across the fields, and out of every hedge you walk up, rabbits run in all directions, you shoot at everything in sight. Some you hit, some you miss, but at the end of the day you go home with a good bag and a sense of satisfaction.'

I had agreed that it was so.

'Now,' he had continued, 'you go on to the next farm, similar to the first, and there's not a bird in sight – no pheasants, no partridges, not even a pigeon. You put your dog into a hedge, and nothing comes out. You're sure that something ought to be there, but the more you search for it, the less is found.

'At this point, you're so sure you've missed something, you go up and down that hedge again and again. The fact that you've found nothing makes you convinced that that rabbit is there somewhere, and you're not going home till you've found it.'

It was logical, I admitted.

'These people are just the same,' he said. 'Give the b – – – – – s some rabbits to shoot at.'

'Yes,' I'd said.

'This is one here,' nodding in the direction of Kenneth Woodman, the farm safety officer, who coincidentally happened to be visiting, and whose visit had provoked Sir Percy's advice. 'See those old power scythes over there? Real man killers. They're his rabbits. I chuck oil over them occasionally, to keep them looking as if I might use them. He leaps up and down over them to such an extent, he forgets to look at the rest.'

It had sounded very good advice. Old Joe had made sure there were plenty of rabbits, in his passion for restoring old and antique machinery.

A shotgun certificate renewal seemed like a very good rabbit.

'Certainly, I can do that,' I said into the phone. 'Just drop it in when you're passing, and I'll sign it for you.'

'Can I do it now?' he said. 'It's overdue, and I'd like it to be at the police station for Monday.'

I thought of the farm meeting about to take place. Signing my name to a shotgun licence application form would take all of twenty seconds. He would see we were busy, and not stop.

'OK,' I said into the phone, 'but come now, before they all come for our farm conference.'

I walked back into the kitchen. Roy and Mary, the publicans, had arrived, full of bonhomie and the latest funny story. Ruth handed them coffee, as the others fell about laughing.

I was about to tell them to come through into my study when they sat down.

Mary saw the prescription pad.

'Do me a favour,' she smiled at me. 'Give me some of my regulars, save me coming to the surgery.'

'All right, are you?' I asked, as I finished writing Bob's prescription, and started on hers. She still suffered from hot flushes, and had for years taken a small dose of female hormone to control it. Regularly, at every consultation, I tried to reduce the dose. Inevitably, she complained that I was too mean, and asked for more.

'Not really,' she said, utterly predictably. 'Can I have the bigger ones this time?'

'No,' I said, 'these are quite big enough.'

'Roy's sleeping pills. He's nearly out.'

I wrote another prescription.

Frank and Joe arrived more or less together, seated themselves at the table, and waited for the kettle to reboil.

'Thank goodness there's one I don't have to medicate,' I thought, looking at Frank, but I was receiving unhappy vibes. Nothing specific, but I was aware he was not happy. I looked at Joe, and nodded to the prescription pad.

'Yes please,' he nodded back.

Joe had developed a little sugar in his water. Two hundred and fifty milligrams of diabinese daily kept him sugar-free. I wrote out the prescription for these, and some more testing sticks. Wordlessly, he passed his urine testing chart over the table to me. It was fine. I passed it back, with the prescription.

The door bell rang. I went to answer it. It was Kenneth Woodman.

'Come in,' I said, holding out my hand for his licence application.

Diffidently he came in.

Uniform, status, badges of office, give a man a dignity. As a farm safety officer, inspecting our worn-out machinery, he was one thing. As a patient, asking a favour, on a Sunday morning, he was another. Normally, he stood erect, upright, his clothes not really other than a natural part of himself, unobtrusive.

Now, I was aware that his hat seemed too big, pulled too

201

far down his face. His small moustache, normally a clipped, neat, military thing, now seemed unkempt and straggly. The collar of his mac was turned up. The whole coat seemed too big and too long, giving him the appearance of a seedy private detective.

He walked into the room, holding the licence application form in his hand. I reached out for it.

He looked round the room.

'Can I speak to you a moment?'

'Of course,' I said.

'Alone, in private.'

'Come into my study,' I said.

We went through into the other room. He did not sit down. The fire blazed in the hearth, the chairs were laid out ready for the meeting. We left the smell of roasting meat and coffee behind.

'You're quite happy to sign this?' he asked. 'You know I tried to kill myself a few years ago?'

'No,' I said, 'I did not. Tell me about it.'

He looked around, embarrassed. 'I'm not sure where to start.'

'Sit down,' I said.

He sat, a solitary figure in a row of chairs. I had had a background awareness that all was not well in his marriage. Nothing had been said, but his wife had consulted me on several occasions over trivia, and I had been aware at the time that she was unhappy, although she had never volunteered any information. Equally, his consultations had been about the mundane, the unimportant, and when, in his capacity as farm safety officer, he had called, I had never actually been involved. I had merely been informed of his verdicts afterwards.

'When was it, and how?' I asked.

He looked very uncomfortable.

'Three years ago. I took an overdose of sleeping pills. Both ladies had found out about each other. It seemed the only way.'

202

'Neither Mac nor I have ever given you any sleeping pills,' I said quietly. 'Where did you get them from?'

'From my other doctor.'

'What other doctor?'

'The one in Norfolk.'

I must have looked suitably confused.

'You mean you don't know?'

'No. Know what?' I asked.

'I,' he said, looking very apologetic, 'travel a lot in my job. My area covers most of Norfolk and Suffolk. My wife lives here, but when I'm away, it seems reasonable to live in one area at a time. I ... I ... have several ladies who accommodate me when I'm in their area. Only two really, my wife, and the other one.' He paused. 'Naturally, when it's offered, you take it, don't you?'

'Go on,' I said, after a while.

'The other lady found out about an affair I was having with someone else. She didn't know I was married either. Things got very difficult. You see, I spend half my time up there, and half down here. I have another doctor up there. I see him periodically. He gave me the pills.'

'Then what happened?' I asked.

'They both threw me out. I went to the third lady. Her husband came home. It was very difficult.'

He looked up at me.

'I was at my wits' end, I didn't know what to do ... It was affecting my work, wandering about, no clean clothes, no sleep.'

He looked down at the shotgun application form in his hand.

'I rang up the office, my wife, the other lady, and the one who threw me out, and told them all I was going to end it.'

'Then what did you do?'

'I drove on for a bit, found a lay-by. I thought that, having told them all, I might just as well do it, so I took out my bottle of sleeping pills and swallowed the lot. It was easy, really.'

'Did you think of using your shotgun?'

'Yes, but it would have been so messy, so awful for them to have to clean up.'

'That was three years ago. Have you had your shotgun ever since?'

'No. The police super advised me not to keep it at home. I leave it with a farmer friend. He keeps it for me, I only have it when we go out actually shooting.'

'Several times a year?'

'More than that, probably every other week.'

'So you've had ample opportunity to shoot yourself, if you were going to, since then?'

'Yes.'

'Are you going to?'

'No.'

'You'll feel safe with a shotgun in the house?'

'Yes.'

It was the classic story of a suicidal gesture, not a real attempt. A cry for help, informing all those involved he was going to try, subconsciously making sure that he would be found.

I looked at the application form. I only had to countersign that he was known to me for more than two years, and that his name and address were correct. Nothing about his suitability to have a licence. That was a police decision.

'Your wife took you back, then? I didn't know anything about this.'

'Yes. I had no choice.' He shrugged his shoulders helplessly. 'Family blackmail. It's the other one I want, but . . .'

'You had no choice.'

It explained a lot of things. I countersigned his application. There was no point in doing otherwise.

Handing it back to him, I opened the door and showed him out. The smell of roasting meat wafted into the hall.

We walked into the kitchen. Ruth was indeed cooking in the farm office. I shepherded him through and out to the back door. Slowly, I shut the door behind me, and turned to face her.

'Shall I move them through?' I mouthed silently.

Resignedly, she shook her head.

'Lunch is almost ready,' she said.

I returned to my place at the table. They had already decided that they must have a farm shop, and to use it all the year round, they would have to lengthen the selling season.

Bedding plants had been suggested. Old George would grow them.

'Bananas,' said Bob. 'Look, here's the catalogue. The seeds are quite cheap, and if you grow them initially in heat, once they've germinated they'll grow quite happily as a pot plant indoors. Banana plants will really sell well.'

The phone rang. I answered it. The labour ward at the hospital: a panic, no one else within reach.

'We know you're not on duty, but can you come, please, quickly?'

I went, agreeing as I did so that we were going to start a garden centre, to complement the farm shop.

Ruth carried on her cooking, in the farm office.

Frank, the only one who was not a patient of mine, looked up.

'Doctor,' he said, 'I've got this great big thorn down the base of my finger, and I can't get it out.'

'When I get back,' I said. 'When I get back.'

MORE TALES FROM A COUNTRY PRACTICE

Arthur Jackson

Continuing the richly entertaining episodes in the life of a young country doctor.

As the red glow of dawn spreads across the sky, Doctor Jackson stands at his bedroom window watching the migrant Canada geese flying in to alight on his lake. He has spent the night answering emergency calls to the holiday camps up the coast, and now here are more temporary residents who are likely to cause him and his collection of rare waterfowl nothing but trouble . . .

But this endearing country doctor, to whom all things are possible, still manages to put his patients first, and their problems and eccentricities keep him fully occupied. Rich with warmth, sparkling with humour and enthusiasm, these tales are as fresh and invigorating as the gentle breeze of a summer's days.

'*A charming reminiscence written with humour and vitality*'
Publishing News

And don't miss Arthur Jackson's delightful
TALES FROM A COUNTRY PRACTICE
also available in Sphere Books

0 7474 0071 7
GENERAL FICTION

Sphere now offers an exciting range of quality fiction and non-fiction by both established and new authors. All of the books in this series are available from good bookshops, or can be ordered from the following address:

Sphere Books
Cash Sales Department
P.O. Box 11
Falmouth
Cornwall TR10 9EN.

Please send cheque or postal order (no currency), and allow 60p for postage and packing for the first book plus 25p for the second book and 15p for each additional book ordered up to a maximum charge of £1.90 in U.K.

B.F.P.O. customers please allow 60p for the first book, 25p for the second book plus 15p per copy for the next 7 books, thereafter 9p per book.

Overseas customers including Eire please allow £1.25 for postage and packing for the first book, 75p for the second book and 28p for each subsequent title ordered.